THE GROWTH HACKER

THE GROWTH HACKER

99 Facts About Personal Growth That Will Make You Think Twice

Muneer Amayoor

BookMedia Publishing House
Pondicherry, 605001, India

BookMedia

BOOKMEDIA PUBLISHING HOUSE INDIA PVT. LTD.
www.bookmedia.com
info@bookmedia.co

ISBN: 978-81-949511-9-3

First published, December 2020;
Published by BookMedia Publishing House India Pvt Ltd

This book is dedicated to

YOU

CONTENTS

PRAISE FOR THE BOOK

"Crisp and to the point...like an arrow which is so well pointed, it hits the target right away!

Dr. Anuradha Mohan
M. B. B. S., M. F Hom. London.
Certified Clinical Cardiologist

"Muneer has perfectly mixed the personal experience with powerful lessons to educate and inspire the readers."

Muhammed Shafeeq Ambalakkunnan
Valuepreneur
M.D Syfex India Pvt. Ltd.

"Offering a marvellous transformational journey, this book is worth reading, internalizing, implementing and reflecting on..."

Rasheed P
Associate Director
Watermelon Communications, Dubai

"A jewel box of experiences, stories and reflections... Muneer Amayoor unearths that diamond within you."

T. Jagadeesh Babu,
Lec. in English
Penna College of Cement Sciences

"Aesop for the modern times...Tightly packed with sentences full of wisdoms for life, the book reminds of the stardust we are made of"

Ami Rasheed
Certified Education Specialist, Dubai

"Just the stimulant we all seek...Combining stories from every walk of life, Muneer Amayoor compels you to be yours best self."

Kamalesh S V
Infopreneur

"By forcing you out of your shell, the book makes you more disciplined, develop better habits and find greatness within you."

Anil Datla
Head of UKEU Talent Acquisition
Qualient Solutions UK Ltd.

"An awesome read! Real life moral stories for our time."

Shafeeq Pulapadan
Speed Reading Coach

FOREWORD BY FAROOKH SENSEI

> "Success is a lifelong journey, hard to begin and easy to give up. The decision to continue the journey depends on you."
>
> ~ Farookh Sensei

It gives me immense pleasure to write the foreword for this book, ***The Growth Hacker: 99 facts about personal growth that will make you think twice***. You see, coachees and mentees come in droves and then go off to achieve fabulous results but only a handful succeed in documenting it. When Muneer allowed me to read his book, it made me so proud and gave me so much of joy.

There is a big difference between taking what you know and using it for your benefit only and taking what you know and sharing it and I commend anyone who makes the effort to share what they have learnt. If we all understood the benefit of sharing, we would realize that our communities would develop exponentially over a short period of time.

Muneer understands that vision and through his nature has committed himself to sharing what he knows through this professionally written book. Written in the simplest style, this book is easy to read. More importantly it has the power of influence, the kind of influence needed to get anyone up from whatever slumber they are in and prepare to meet their challenges.

What makes the book special also is that it is written from a pure perspective because it has a combination of the personal and professional experiences of Muneer. Perspectives like these are powerful because they come from a ***"tried and tested"*** place. I am not purporting that what has worked for one person will work for everyone. However, starting from some place that someone has tried is better than having to start from no place at all.

I have also always maintained that story telling is a powerful place from which to educate others. It has always been a crowd puller and I think it will never change. Grandparents tell it to grandkids to educate by entertaining them. Parents read bedtime stories to their children before tucking them into bed. Tribal folk tell stories by campfires at night to lend perspectives from forefathers. Today, public speakers tell stories on stage in order to get audiences to resonate with them. But the beauty of story telling through book writing is that they remain engrained in our mind without ever getting erased or forgotten. They can always be accessed and read again. They can be shared easily, and their messages can be learnt from, consistently.

The Growth Hacker, 99 facts about personal growth that will make you think twice is a book like that. It is a book that can be read, shared, gifted, and kept close by. It's a collection of wonderful lessons you will want to go back to repeatedly to get your spirits up and to motivate yourself to stay focused and committed always.

It is my fervent prayer also that those who read this book will be inspired to come forward and write their own books to share and develop their communities. We are living at a time when the phrase ***"sharing is caring"*** is extremely relevant and necessary. Reading books are now a necessity rather than a luxury.

Thrive and help others thrive too.

Farookh Sensei
Founder and CEO of Ledge International
www.farookhsensei.com

ACKNOWLEDGMENTS

All praise be to the God Almighty.

Farookh Sensei

I am deeply indebted to you forever for motivating me, for your persuasive mentoring and for igniting the fire within me. Thank you so much for the beautifully written forward for this book. I couldn't think of a better person to do write the forward. Thank you.

Maqsood P

Thank you for your marvellous editing and polishing work. Without the sleepless nights you spent, this book couldn't have been as beautiful as it is now.

Valuepreneur Shafeeq

Thank you for constantly enquiring about the progress and motivating me to stay on track.

Zaid Benadra

Thank you for the beautiful cover design. Thanks to your service, the book could boast of an appealing cover.

Shibu PM, Paurnami Chitran

Thank you for the brilliant promotions you designed. They will go a long way in furthering the book's outreach.

My parents, wife, brothers, colleagues, relatives, friends, teachers, students, radio listeners and all well- wishers

Thank you so much for making me who I am today and for extending your heartfelt support along the way.

To you

Thank you for giving me this opportunity to serve you.

INTRODUCTION

The intention behind this endeavour is not to motivate but rather to transform whoever goes through the whole book. Designed nothing like a cliched 'motivational' read, the entire work is drawn from my life experiences, thoughts and feelings. Motivational advice is the last thing to expect from this book, it's, simply, not my cup of tea. What one would do with pieces of advice that will never come in handy?

The idea of writing this book struck me while I was doing a course under the guidance of Farookh Sensei, a wonderful coach for leadership empowerment. It all began when I engaged myself in jotting down my concepts and convictions on personal growth in the form of quotations. The original plan was to publish these quotes of mine in the form of a book. However I could not hold myself back from expanding each quote to further paragraphs. Once the gear was shifted, thoughts made marks on the paper and this book was born. It was a slow and gradual evolution. The old photographs stored in my personal devices helped me walk down the memory lane and supplied me with enough materials to communicate my perceptions in the simplest way.

Great effort has been taken to avoid any jargons or rhetoric so as to strike a chord with the readers of any walk of life. My aim is that any person, school kid, layman, CEO, entrepreneur, whoever happens to come across this book should be able to read this without much effort.

Muneer Amayoor

PART ONE

MOVE FORWARD

1 TAKE CALCULATED RISKS

Will you resign from a peaceful and a high-paying job? That too, when you have no other immediate job prospects at hand. Will you dare doing that? Well, that's what I did.

When I resigned from my first central government job as a Postal Assistant, I was deemed to be naive by some of my dear friends and relatives. They cannot be blamed; such a central government job is only an elusive dream job for many. Besides, the competition is extremely tight. I had no other job at that time. My mind told me that I should not continue for a long time in that clerical post where there were comparatively fewer challenges and minimal room for creativity. I felt that I would be confined to a tiny little comfortable box with virtually no challenges to push myself. It was a tough decision to make. However, I thought, I would rather be a risk-taker than a file-pusher in a comfy chair. However, my superior's eyebrows went crazy when I handed my resignation letter only 16 months after joining.

People around me found my future plan even more stupid. Intriguingly stupid. Pursuing Post Graduation, M.Tech. in Computer Science was my plan at the time. Given that I had failed in the M.Tech. entrance tests twice already, people had reasons to raise their eyebrows, I guess. But this time, thanks to my sheer hard work and resolve, I was able to clear the cut-off and joined M.Tech. By then, I was done with being an average student, I set a definite goal for myself and decided that I would qualify the UGC NET in Computer Science, which would qualify me to be a University Professor. A guy who had failed in Computer Science entrance test, that too twice, and then pursuing UGC NET in the same subject may seem to be an ultra-unrealistic dream. However, to the astonishment of many of my friends and mentors, not only did I qualify UGC NET in the subject, I also qualified for JRF (Junior Research Fellowship). And that too, in my very first attempt when I was still a M.Tech. student. On top of that, at that time, I was one among the only four people in Kerala, who had qualified for JRF in the Computer Science.

I worked as a Soft Skills Trainer for school students for one year after M.Tech. Then I joined All India Radio as a Programme Producer and Presenter. I would say, it was a turning point. Speaking was my passion, and here, I get paid for speaking. I get paid for doing what I love the most.

Along with that, I started to speak to students and professionals and helped them in their personal growth. Now, on the online platform Udemy, I have students from 117 different countries.

> "Life is either a daring adventure or nothing at all."
>
> \- Helen Keller

Just think, where would I be now, if I had decided to stick with my first job? Ask yourself, are you following your mind? Some decisions are tough and risky, but if you want to grow, have the courage to take calculated risks.

> "A right decision at the right time, no matter how tough, takes you to the right destination."
>
> \- Muneer Amayoor

2 STEP OUT OF YOUR COMFORT ZONE

"Eyes on the road! Don't look down. I told you, it's A-B-C from the right. Accelerator, break and clutch... keep your eyes on the road."

My driving instructor was a bit furious as I kept looking down every time I wanted to change the gear. All of you must have similar experiences that you remember. Nervously taking your seat behind the steering wheel for the first time, holding tight onto the steering wheel, driving with all your concentration focused on the road, having a little heart attack every time another vehicle passed by and your legs nervously shaking on the clutch pedal. All of them are relatable.

Yet, from such an awkward driver most of you graduated to the expert level. Right? It was not an easy going, was it? Imagine now how easily you drive through those serpentine roads, how easily you navigate your way through a heavy traffic and how easily you park your car in a tiny spot. But, it was not like that always, was it? Once, you had preferred only straight roads, you had taken time-consuming detours to avoid heavily trafficked roads, you used to dread having to make a gear shift while climbing a steep road and properly parking your car used to be a headache for you.

Now, ask yourself, would you have become an expert driver you are today, if you never had dared taking curvy roads? No. Afraid of making a gear shift amidst a climb, if you never had tried climbing, would you have become an expert in climbing steep roads? No. If you had never dared driving through a busy road, wouldn't you still be an amateur driver? Yes. An easy road never makes a good driver, nor does a calm sea make an expert sailor. A favourable sky without winds or clouds, could never make an expert pilot.

Your actual growth starts, only when you step out of your comfort zone. Push yourself out of your comfort zone and have the courage to challenge yourself. If you are presented only with favorable conditions, you will not get an opportunity to become your best version. You might know how the dull looking carbon turns into precious diamonds. Carbon turns into precious diamond only if it is subjected to extremely high pressure and temperature.

"I know God will not give me anything I can't handle. I just wish that He didn't trust me so much."

- Mother Teresa

Next time you are faced with an insurmountable pressure, ask yourself, "Do I want to miss this opportunity to turn myself into a shining diamond?".

"Hardships come with an opportunity to transform yourself into your best version."

- Muneer Amayoor

3 PURPOSE MATTERS

John was a school teacher. Once, when he got selected for a contest in a TV quiz show, he was not expecting much. Naturally, when he somehow reached the finals, not only did he feel totally bemused, he felt that he was living in an alternative surreal world! The prize money was a whopping ₹500 million. The day came, and the contest started. John had never been more nervous in his life. After a series of nerve-racking rounds, to his own surprise, John made it to the final question. His answer to the question would be the unreal difference between winning ₹500 million, or losing it. The stakes were high, his heart was pounding, the air felt thin, the hall stood still, John uttered his answer and he won the whopping prize of ₹500 million.

What do you think would happen to John now? Will he succeed in his life? Will the prize change his life for good?

He went home with the money. Many relatives and friends, many of them were not to be seen for years, suddenly appeared out of nowhere and acted as if they knew John from the past life itself. Many came knocking on his door seeking help and many of them were not genuine either. However, John had no plan for his newly earned riches. He sought no counsel from any financial expert. Instead, he started spending money without a thought. He bought everything his eyes saw. Besides, he became a local celebrity. He got invitations to take part in many inaugural programmes and cultural events. In the meantime, he forgot that he once had a job, and now he has no job at hand. Having lost any sense of purpose in his life, he turned to drugs as well. His wife was totally disappointed by her husband's abusive behavior and irrational management of money. When she had enough of it and she could no longer stand his treatment, she went to her house, packing up her stuff. Addicted to drugs, John had barely been sober enough to notice his wife's absence.

It did not take long for John to run out of money and go bankrupt. But with his all new-found "joys", he could no longer go back to his old life. He had forgotten that once he was a teacher satisfied with his lot. To keep up his rich-man's reputation, he turned to bank loans. Years passed as a he lead a life of luxury and riches. In occasional brief moments of sobriety and clarity, he genuinely wept for what happened in his life, his family, his peace and how his life had turned upside down. To forget the pain, he would turn to drugs again.

Several years later, one night, he woke up with a feeling of absolute meaninglessness and fear. In the next few still-hours of absolute dread, his thoughts went crazy. He asked himself, deeper questions about the meaning and purpose of his life. In his current life, he could find none. No meaning, no purpose, no destination. Tears welled up in eyes, he wept like a child, memories of his past life-a happy teacher, a loving husband-flashed across his mind. And in a rare moment of painful clarity, he was able to appreciate how he won the million dollar prize and how it turned his life upside down. He was suddenly able to realise that, it was because he lost sight of any purpose that he lost himself in the illusions of alcohol and luxury. A million times, he imagined how things could have gone if he had put his money to good use to help himself and those around him. Overwhelmed by a deep sense of shame and repentance that shook him from head to toe, slowly and gradually, he slipped into a deep sleep.

The next day, he woke up wiser and determined. He wanted to take his life back to his control and he realised that the first thing he needed was a job. After a lot of efforts, knocking on several doors, appealing to many, finally, he could get a job in a school as a teacher. The salary was comparatively less, but at least he was sober and with it returned hope, peace, purpose and his wife. Life became meaningful and prosperous.

> "Good luck is another name for tenacity of purpose."
>
> - Ralph Waldo Emerson

What is your purpose in life? In which direction are you headed now? What will you do if you had 100 times more money than that you have now? Try to see the bigger picture with a sense of purpose.

> "A person without purpose is like an aeroplane out of control."
>
> - Muneer "Purpose Matters" Amayoor

4 COMMANDER MIND

Going back to the college where you once studied is always a joyous experience. But, what if you return to your college as a Guest of Honour? How many of us have daydreamt about such a heroic return to our alma mater?

I was fortunate enough to have such experiences, not once, but several times. First of such experiences was when I was once invited as a guest to the College of Engineering, Munnar, where I had studied for my graduation. Another one was when I was invited to the MES College of Engineering, Kuttippuram, where I had studied for my post graduation. Please do not think that I am bragging about my achievements, but believe me, the experience was exceptionally delighting.

Apart from being the Guest of Honour, I was tasked with igniting the spark in the students. I believe that everyone has some sort of a spark in them; it just needs the right weapon to be ignited. At both campuses, I used my favourite weapon of ignition. Hypnosis.

Volunteers were invited onto the stage and they were given instructions to make themselves feel relaxed and fall to a deep state of sleep. Once under my hypnotic control, I started playing with their mind. I told Neha, that her feet were super heavy that she could not walk when she opens her eyes. Then I asked her to open her eyes.

I told her, "Try to walk".

She tried, but failed, and looked at my eyes, perplexed.

"Try to walk, but you can't. The more you try, the more stuck you will be. Your feet weigh 1000 pounds.", I said.

She tried her best to walk, but she was completely stuck.

"If you manage to move at least an inch, I would give you this cash." I took out a currency note from my wallet and said. Again, she failed to walk, then, I told her, "If you move your feet at least an inch, I would give you the entire money in this wallet."

Again, she tried, but her legs were petrified, fixed like a rock, unable to budge an inch.

As the audience were laughing, I told her, "When I clap my hands, you will fall asleep, but you will not fall back, your legs will support you!"

Then I said in a commanding voice,"Sleep!"

At that very next moment, she closed her eyes and slept standing upright.

Are you wondering what happened here? I will reveal that secret for you.

In a hypnotic state, the subject is brought to a relaxed state through suggestions. In that state, the hypnotist is talking to the subconscious mind of the person. The mind believes whatever the Hypnotist says, and the body obeys the suggestions.

This happens not only in a hypnotic state, but all the time. What you believe in your mind is reflected outward. If you think you are weak, your body becomes weak. If you think that you are strong, your body becomes strong. The underlying beliefs in your mind decide who you are. Simply put, you are what you think you are!

How are these beliefs formed in your mind? To answer that question, we would have to take an epic journey back to your mother's womb. Yes, your mind gets programmed right from the womb itself. The experiences, words and actions of your mother influence you. During the pregnancy, everything she does, everything she says and everything she undergoes have a profound effect on the way your mind evolves. Once you are born and start living in this complex society, parents, teachers, friends and even the grocery shop keeper you meet, play a big role in programming your mind as you grow. Above all, your own thoughts and actions have a profound impact on your mind and the way your body responds to everything.

If there is any belief in your mind which limits your horizon or if there is any thought residing in your mind which makes you feel weak, it is time to re-programme your mind. It is time to reinvent yourself. It is time to stop your mind from being your own enemy. Tell yourself that you are strong. Record it in your own voice and listen to it every day. Repeat this technique until it works its magic. Once you are able to make your mind believe in it, it is easier to make it real.

> "Winners make a habit of manufacturing their own positive expectations in advance of the event."
>
> – Brian Tracy

Now ask yourself, what is that self-limiting belief you have in your mind? If you want to grow to your full potential, you ought to say goodbye to it. Right now. Ask yourself, do you want to grow to your full potential? You know what to do!

> "You are what your mind commands."
>
> - Muneer Amayoor

5 CONNECT TO LEAD

He came to that company with prodigious experience from several other reputed corporate companies. His resume was filled with a lot of qualifications and projects he had undertaken. The management was very hopeful that he will join their company to lead the team in the right direction.

He was very skilled and confident, so he did not seek opinion from his team members before taking major decisions. However, all the decisions were right ones. He made every member accountable for their work and meticulously monitored them. He was working 24x7, monitoring the progress every moment. The company witnessed a sharp growth at that time. Naturally, he grew more and more confident and made important right decisions himself. None of the team members, not even senior members were consulted with or convinced by his moves.

After a few months, gradually, two groups developed among the staff members; one group of hardworking employees, and another group of aloof employees who stood back from everything and felt that they are not part of the company anymore. Many senior staff shrunk to themselves, stayed back from their duties, and started to look for new opportunities in other avenues.

> "The challenge of leadership is to be strong, but not rude; be kind, but not weak; be bold, but not a bully; be thoughtful, but not lazy; be humble, but not timid; be proud, but not arrogant; have humor, but without folly."
>
> – Jim Rohn

In the long run, will this company survive with this mode of leadership? When making decisions, do you think that convincing your team members is also important?

> "A leader is a connector; connector of different souls for an inspiring mission with a powerful vision."
>
> - Muneer Amayoor

6 BE A PASSIONPRENEUR

Do you believe that hard work is the way to success? If you believe so, get up from your seat, go near to the wall and push it as hard as you can. Try it! Does it work?

If not hard work, is smart work the best way to success? Haven't you seen young adults working exceptionally smart, hitting their timeframe and goals and keeping their boss happy? However, in the long run, can you see all of them successful? I mean, success in the sense that, do you feel that they are really content with their work and life? Mostly, no.

Then, what is the secret ingredient to stay actually happy and productive at work? Passion is the secret ingredient which makes your work fruitful in the long run. Apple became a No.1 company, because its founder, Steve Jobs founded the company out of passion. Similarly, a farmer will be super happy if he is working in the field with passion. Let's call it the "heart work". At the same time, do all those who work with passion reach their goals? No!

Combining smartness with the heart work is the secret recipe to reap enduring success. Set a time frame for your passionate work and design ways to leverage your time and money. Evolve as a passionpreneur.

> "I have no special talents. I am only passionately curious."
>
> - Albert Einstein

What are the five things you should do now, to accelerate your journey to become a passionpreneur?

> "Neither hard work, nor smart work, but 'heart work' keeps you at the top."
>
> - Muneer Amayoor

7 MANTRA FOR JOB INTERVIEW

One fine Sunday morning, My father and I were sitting out with a cup each of warm black tea in our hand. Somehow, our discussion turned to his first ever interview experience. “Do you know what happened at my first ever job interview?”, lifting his face up to meet mine, he asked. Steam from the warm tea-cup had visibly blurred his glasses. “No, I don’t. Tell me what happened?”, said I. As our conversation progressed, he revealed that one of the questions that the interview panel had asked was ridiculously easy to answer. ‘They asked me, “What year was it?”. Son, I was taken aback by the question’, said my Father. I thought to myself, how stupid the interview panel had to be to ask a question as simple as that. Then, my father revealed what happened afterwards. He panicked, his mind went blank, he felt numb, and he blurted out the wrong answer. It was with a visible smile of embarrassment on his face, that he revealed how he had failed to answer such a simple question in his first ever interview.

Can you guess, why my father's first ever interview went terribly wrong? Can you guess why he could not answer such a simple question?

This experience is quite relatable to many. I have heard many graduates complaining about how they panicked at their first interview. For some, not just the first interview, every interview is a nightmare. Recently, a post graduate in English approached me to overcome her terrible fear of interview. "My interview is the day after, but, I already have butterflies in my stomach", she said.

Exactly, what is happening here? First, remember that it happens not only with fresh college graduates, but with some experienced professionals as well. As a matter of fact, when someone is worried, he/she loses the ability to think clearly. If he is too much concerned about the outcome of the interview, it will reflect in their interview performance. What does it mean? Does it mean that one has to go to the interview hall without any preparation? No! Absolutely, no! Prepare well, prepare particularly for the anticipated questions. Preparation is the key for a stellar performance at an interview

All your preparations will go in vain if you do not overcome the fear in the first place. So, how can you overcome the fear? The best way to overcome the fear is to reprogramme your mind with a self-affirmation, "I don't need this job, the company needs my expertise and service. I am the fittest person for this job. Let them decide whether or not they are worthy of my service." I am not asking you to be arrogant nor to be over-confident, instead I am asking you to develop self-respect and dignity that most candidates tend to leave outside the interview hall. It is not you who needs the company's assistance; it is the company that needs your expertise and service. Never ever beg for the job. Develop a sense of self-respect. Give yourself the respect you deserve! When you enter the interview hall with this mindset, you get an upper hand. Do not beg for job. Give yourself some respect!

A few days before the interview, you can record a voice file in your mobile phone which should go like this: "Muneer, you are the fittest person for the job. The company needs your service. You need not worry. If the company needs your service, you will get the job. Else, they lose a valuable employee"

Now, let me reveal something. In almost every interview I attended with this mindset, I was selected.

"To be a great champion, you must believe you are the best. If you're not, pretend you are."

- Muhammad Ali

Now, how are you going to attend your next interview? As frightened beggar? Or as valuable employee that the company could not afford to lose? The decision is yours to make.

" 'I don't need the job, it is them who need my unparalleled service' – this is the Mantra for job interviews."

- Muneer Amayoor

8 VISUALISE THAT CUSTOMER YOU TARGET

If you had a chest pain, would you go to a General Practitioner or a Cardiologist? If a Cardiologist is available, you would definitely go to him, right? Specialists are always in high demand.

If you are into business, training or any other field, identify your niche. Narrow the niche to explicitly target your customer. Your services and products should be custom-tailored for the needs of a specific section of the demography. For that, first you have to precisely identify and define your target customer. Ask yourself; what will be the age, character traits, spending habits, annual income, and favourite books/movies/shows of your ideal customers? Who is your customer avatar? Identify one person, who would fit to the descriptions of your ideal customer. See that person in mind, and design your product/service exclusively for him/her. Sure, if you tailor your marketing strategy to fit your target customers precisely, you will definitely be headed for success in your niche.

By selecting a niche, you are not only treated as an expert, but this strategy also leaves you with virtually no competitors. Besides, it cuts down your spending advertisement by large as you have to target only a narrow demographic section, thereby saving money and effort.

> *"Commit to a niche;* Try to *stop being* everything to everyone."
>
> \- Andrew Davis

I know what you are thinking about now! "What is my niche?", right? You have spent more time with yourself than with anyone else in the world. That means, no one knows you better than you do! So, pause for a second, close your eyes and find answers to the following questions. What kind of problems have you solved for yourself and others? To which person can you relate the most? What makes you motivated? If you find answers to these questions, you know what and where your niche is. Also, consider whether your niche is relevant in terms of business.

> "Visulise your ideal customer in your mind and tailor your product to fit him."
>
> \- Muneer Amayoor

9 RESTART NOW!

With a restart button right next to the power button, restarting your PC is not a big deal. But not restarting your life. One of the hardest things in life is restarting something we have left halfway through. But, in the unpredictable life of ours, we are forced to leave many of our long-term goals halfway through.

Once, a 30 year old woman was called to our talk show programme at the Manjeri FM radio. She was an unemployed home-maker and initially, she did not sound special in anyway. She sounded simply like a regular house-wife. But, once she opened her heart about her dream and the plan for the upcoming years, we got a taste of how strong a lady she was. She revealed that she was married off early in her teenage and that she was forced to drop her studies immediately afterwards. Every time she opened her books for studying, her in-laws would cast a disgusting look at her and it was later that she came to learn that it was part of the "marriage deal" between her family and in-laws that she was not to continue her studies after the marriage. Having been denied every opportunity to learn and grow, she is now a mother to four children and she had called to the talk-show in order to publicly announce her strong will and decision to continue her higher studies at the age of 30. "The wings of my dreams were once cut off and now I decide to fly again, I'll make my own wings." She said. I was reminded of the mythical character, Daedalus who was trapped in a labyrinth and devised a pair of wings for himself in order to make his escape from the labyrinth.

After long years, she is now determined to resume her studies and join for higher secondary course. She was determined to break the boundaries set around her, expand her horizon, follow the lost dreams, and prove to the world that it is never too late to take your life into your hands and give a shot at your dreams again. She further said that she would ensure that her girl child gets a fair chance to study and chase her ambitions. Over the years, I have known countless women like this lady, who resumed their studies long after it came to a sudden halt with their marriage. They announce with their resounding voice that, it is better to restart late, than never restarting.

"Your life does not get better by chance. It gets better by change."

- Jim Rohn

Do you have any dream that you were forced to drop along the way? If yes, do you have the courage and willpower to tell the world that you cannot be bound in chains? It is never late, my friend. Chase your dream. It is never late.

> "If hope is in the driving seat, a new way appears when it seems like a dead end."
> - Muneer Amayoor

10 EMOTION TRIGGERS GROWTH

Sometimes, people who are hell-bent on disrupting your life, end up helping you like no one else. It may not be what they have intended, but sadly for them, they end up playing a crucial role in our growth.

After the M.Tech, confused by the choices I was presented with, I was being pulled in all directions. All India Radio on the one side, PhD. options on the other, and an attractive job offer by the Tata Consultancy Services-which one should I choose? My mind told me to follow my passion which is, undoubtedly, speaking and writing. Finally, following my passion, I decided to join All India Radio.

I joined at AIR, Thrissur, and with passion started working there. Initially, I did not know that daunting challenges were waiting for me in queue. Once, one person, who was an office-bearer of an organisation called me on phone and asked me to never broadcast in my own voice. He pointed out that my voice was the worst, not fit for broadcasting. When I refused to act as he said, he sent a letter to our headquarters at Delhi alleging that my voice is totally unsuitable to be broadcast through All India Radio. However, to my comfort, my colleagues stood with me. I started taking baby steps in programme production with the guidance of my seniors.

Later in the year 2017, I was transferred to AIR, Manjeri, Kerala which happens to be my hometown. It was from Manjeri, where I was pushed to the vast world of radio. When I joined, my station director instructed me, "Muneer, you may produce radio programmes here, but please do not broadcast in your own voice." My eyes wet, throat dried. Still, I said, "Yes, sir."

After a few days, I did one thing. I recorded a programme in my own voice and broadcast without seeking permission. After the broadcast was over, Station Director called me to his cabin. I was expecting to see the Director red with rage and yelling at me like a grumpy boss, and I was ready to take it all. I entered the cabin. Surprisingly, he welcomed me with a smile and extended his hand to shake. It was a real shock! He told me, "Muneer, from now on, you must produce programmes and broadcast in your own voice." I could not believe my ears. Seeing the reaction on my face, he smiled and revealed a story.

Before I joined AIR Manjeri, the Director had already got a picture about me. Not at all a good picture!! That was through an article about me published in a magazine with a state-wide circulation. The person, who had earlier sent the complaint against me to Delhi was, understandably, obsessed with me. When he came to know that I will not act as he had rudely suggested, he sent a letter to the magazine, resulting in the publication of a derogatory article about me and my "unsuitable voice". I guess, that person had kept himself quite busy. Because, in addition to the publication of the article, the same person had also sent a letter and a copy of the magazine to every AIR station in Kerala. This was the reason for the "voice ban".

With the guidance of the Director and support from colleagues, I started doing short talks and writing scripts. Gradually, I started compèring live shows and phone-in programmes. Now, I feel proud that almost every day, my voice goes on air and reaches to innumerable listeners all across the state. In time, I have covered programmes of the President, the Prime Minister and the Vice President of India. The unparalleled love bestowed by our listeners makes me fully satisfied.

It is the failures that make you stronger. If someone tries to make you a laughing stock and showers negative criticisms on you, be happy. You will be thankful to them one day, like I am today to that man who sent letters to the AIR stations for igniting the fire within me.

Still, I am facing innumerable challenges on my way, but now I know that Carbon turns into precious diamond only when it is subjected to extremely high pressure and temperature.

> "Any fool can criticize, condemn, and complain but it takes character and self- control to be understanding and forgiving."
>
> \- Dale Carnegie

Look back at your life, don't you realise some of your great achievements were triggered by anger, bullying, sadness or harassment?

> "Some great journeys start with an emotionally charged moment. Let your pain be your trigger."
>
> \- Muneer Amayoor

11 THE WINNING COMMUNICATOR

Recently, I was overwhelmed by a great sense of nostalgia for one of my favourite childhood games when I came to know that some of the popular TV talk-shows are now featuring the same game. You might remember the game, especially if you had an extended family with a lot of cousins with whom you must have played the game. I am talking about charades. As you might know, there are a million ways to play charades, but our favourite one was the one in which the player has to pantomime the title of a movie or an actor and the other members of the team have to guess the title/name. A classic game of doing pantomime to communicate an idea.

Most often, the actors, despite all their best efforts, make themselves a laughing stock. However, in the game every communication and miscommunication adds to its fun. I remember, how once one of my friends tried to pantomime the movie title *Jurassic Park* and acted out the famous nerve-racking scene of the giant T-Rex breaking through the fence and walking towards the car with kids in it. I hope, you remember the scene. However, when my friend tried to act out the T-Rex's walk, with his body slightly bent down and by taking big steps, his teammates immediately mistook it a for Malayalam film titled *Kunjikoonan* which features a protagonist who is a hunch back. You cannot blame the teammates. Though the actor did a good job acting out the T-Rex's walk, the teammates took it for a hunchback's gait. I still remember the awkward smile he had on his face when he finally revealed what he was trying to communicate.

In the game, the actors know what they are trying to communicate and with body movements and facial expressions they try their best to communicate the movie title. Despite their best efforts, like my friend, often they fail to communicate. What is happening when an act of communication fails? Communication fails when the understood meaning is not the same as the intended meaning.

When you play the charades, every miscommunication could be a reason for laughter. The more miserably the actor fails, the more drama and laughter you can expect. But not in the real world. In the real world, far from fun and laughter, miscommunications can lead to arguments, duels, brawls, divorces and even start a war. During the

Crimean War, it was a chain of miscommunications that resulted in the failure of the British military action generally known as the Charge of the Light Brigade. Due to the communication failure, the military move was doomed to fail which resulted in high casualties for the British army. If nothing had gone wrong with the British Army's communication, the military action could have changed the course of war for them. Instead, it resulted in the death of several brave soldiers, causing a major setback for the British forces.

With proper communication, how many divorces could have been averted? With proper communication, how many brawls could have been avoided? If a channel for proper communication with the potential customers was in place, how many more customers could you have won for your business? Communication is an art, an art once you master, could win you more friends, more customers, more business, more peace and what not. Being social animals caught in numerous networks of human communication, we are playing charades every second in our life. The better a communicator you are, the better you can score in your life's game. When you say something, when you write an article, when you draft an order, when you prepare a brochure or even when you say "Hi", the game of communication should be in your mind.

> "People may hear your words, but they feel your attitude."
>
> - John C. Maxwell

Just think, what if your gentle smile is mistaken for mocking? What can you do to make sure that you have communicated your idea correctly? If possible, you may ask the listener if they have understood your point. If it is not possible, before stopping the conversation, you can repeat your key points. And most importantly, never forget to use the lessons from a previous chapter where we talked about how to effectively connect with people.

> "A winning communicator makes sure that the understood message is the photocopy of the intended message."
>
> - Muneer Amayoor

12 GET IT RIGHT!

"What will I do? Nothing is working well. My ads do not bring me customers", the owner of a small dry cleaning centre in India sighed. His college-going son heard his father's predicament. He told his father, "Don't worry Baba, let me handle it the right way".

He wrote on a paper:

"Dear busy women folk,

Are you pressed for the time to get your silk sarees dry cleaned? Is the heap of clothes of your husband and children consuming all your day? Well then, forget your worries; leave it to us, so that you can utilize your quality time more productively and you can have all your time to yourselves! Book now and we will collect the clothes from your home, and deliver them neat and clean, back to you the next day. Get 3 sarees perfectly dry cleaned at just ₹ 299!!"

He made an attractive poster with a picture of sarees, and posted the ad with this text on the Facebook. The target was clear and the message could not be missed. Within a few days, they started to get a lot of orders, beyond their expectations.

What was the need of the new strategy here, and how it helped them? *The boy got it right*- he switched the focus from selling the product to the real problems faced by busy women. That has made all the difference.

"Understanding is the first step to acceptance, and only with acceptance can there be recovery."

- J.K. Rowling

How often do you pause to introspect? And how often do you directly address the roadblocks in your life? Do you get it right as the boy did?

"GROWTH means, to have the courage to constantly judge yourself and seek New Ways until you Get it Right to reach your destination."

-Muneer Amayoor

13 ACCEPT, RECHARGE, RESTART

Do you feel that you are a victim in your life? You may be and you may not be responsible for that. But, let me tell you, if you remain a victim for long, you are responsible for that. You always have an option to take your life into your control. You have.

Once, when I was watching a YouTube video on my phone, suddenly, my phone rang and instantly, my eyes sparkled with joy and surprise. It was one of my former students calling. I was particularly excited, because she was one of the brightest students I ever had and I thought she must have some pleasant news to share. She must have made some incredible achievement and she must be calling to share her delight. In an instant, my thought went crazy about all the possible achievements she must have made. No longer able to hold my curiosity, I picked the call.

"I got divorced. I feel completely lost in my life. What should I do?"

Her words hit my ears like a thunderbolt. She was just nineteen years old. Though her desire was to pursue higher studies, she was forcefully married off at the age of eighteen. She had nodded "yes" only in the eleventh hour when her would-be had guaranteed that she will be allowed to pursue her studies after the marriage. However, the promise remained unfulfilled and soon after her marriage, she was forced by her in-laws to terminate her studies. She felt betrayed and life turned bitter. Making everything worse, soon, he began coming home late, high on alcohol. Her voice was breaking up when she was talking about those dreadful nights when he used to come drunk and used to beat her up. As if that was not enough, soon it came to the light that her husband was having affairs with multiple women. Her life was, literally, turned upside down, it felt more like a nasty episode from a drama series.

She returned to her parents and refused to go back to her in-laws. After a meeting between her in-laws and her family members, it was decided that she would return to her husband if he promises to be a changed man. But nothing lasted long. In another few weeks her husband started to show his true colours again. This time, she was resolved to take her life into her control and filed for a divorce which, eventually, worked out in her favour.

She was one of the brightest students in my class. How would I respond to such a sad news? How could I console her? I told her to assume that she was, in fact, lucky in a sense. She got her life back in control and that it is good that she could get her divorce before they had any children. How worse it would have been if she was left with a child? Would not the ill-luck be carried on to the next generation as well? I asked her to be proud of herself. Because of her timely act, the worst was averted. Besides, I also encouraged her to pursue higher studies and reach a good position."What would be a better revenge, sir?" she said with a smile."Yes, indeed. A sweet revenge", I echoed back. Now, she is a determined student, enthusiastically pursuing her higher studies that were left mid-way through. Whatever happened, happened. She did not choose to spend the rest of her life like a victim. Instead, she turned her tragedy into a fuel to power her way ahead-her way to glory.

If you find yourself in a trouble over which you have virtually no control, is cursing going to help you? Is complaining going to help you? Is turning yourself to a cry-baby going to help you? No. The answer is an affirmative NO. Whatever happened, was destined to happen. There is no way you could change it. But you could change, how you respond to it. Accept whatever has happened and take steps to turn the situation for your benefit at the earliest.

"Without forgetting it is quite impossible to live at all."

- Friedrich Nietzsche

Now, what will you do if something tragic happens to you? Be a cry-baby? Or turn the tragedy into a fuel to push you ahead? Choice is yours. And so is the life, it is yours.

"If you feel down after a big problem, console yourself you got out of the problem before it turned worse."

- Muneer Amayoor

14 MIRROR WITHOUT ERROR

We receive countless number of phone calls to our live phone-in programmes at All India Radio. People from all walks of life-farmers, housewives, entrepreneurs, students, kids, the list goes on- keep calling us. We would engage in a chit-chat and then play their favourite songs. Here, do you know how we connect with all these diverse people? We, actually, connect with their hearts and there is a secret for it.

We talk in their language. If it is a kid calling, the presenter would speak in the kid's language. If it is an old person, the presenter speaks with respect and empathy. If it is a college student, energetic chit-chats take place. Speaking the language of your companion is the best way to make a bridge from your heart to their hearts.

This applies everywhere. Whether you are a teacher, business man, entrepreneur, student, whatever you are, this technique will help you for sure. But, to understand the science behind it, I would advise you to read the next few paragraphs as attentively as you can.

1) Thanks to some new discoveries in the field of Neuro-Linguistics, we know that the best way to connect with your speaking partner is to identify with and mirror the same emotion as your speaking partner's.

Now, you might ask how to identify your speaking partners' emotion. Well, read on.

2) According to Neuro-Linguistics, in order to easily identify anyone's emotion, all you have to do is to pay close attention to their speech and look for clues to identify their Primary Sense.

Now, what is Primary Sense and how it can help you in connecting with people? Primary Sense is a concept in Neuro-Linguistics. Everyone has his/her own preferred Primary Sense. For some, their primary sense may be visual, while for some it may be auditory, and for a few others it may be kinesthetic. You can identify anyone's Primary Sense by paying attention to their language and you can respond accordingly.

For example, the vocabulary of the people with Visual Primary Sense will be more visual in nature while Auditory people may go for words associated with sounds and Kinesthetic people's word choices would reflect their love for actions.

3) To understand it better, take a look at the following questions asked by different people with different Primary Senses:

    a. Generic: Do you agree with my point?

    b. Visual: Do you have the same picture in your mind?

    c. Auditory: Do you resonate with my point?

    d. Kinesthetic: Are you in touch with my point?

All the above points can be boiled down to this: by paying attention to ones' speech you can identify their Primary Sense and emotional inclination, so that we can try to mirror the speaker's emotion using his preferred words which would allow us to connect with the person in no time. It is a trick we employ during every talk show. It works every time.

How can you apply this in your everyday life? Keep reading. It is simple.

When a customer approaches to buy a car, if he is a visual person, show him the visually attractive parts and talk about its visual appeal. He will surely fall for you. If the customer is auditory, demonstrate him how silent the driving experience is. If he is a kinesthetic person, do not waste time talking about its features, ask him to get into the driving seat, fasten the seat belt and experience the driving.

> **"The single biggest problem in communication is the illusion that it has taken place."**
>
> **- George Bernard Shaw**

What is your preferred sense? Observe how you speak, and how you are impacted at certain occasions, then, you can find your preferred mode.

> **"Mirror the language of your companion to connect without error."**
>
> **- Muneer Amayoor**

15 IT'S NOT WHAT IT IS, IT'S HOW YOU RESPOND TO IT

I am writing this chapter when I am in quarantine. If you happen to read this book long after its publication, you might wonder why I was in quarantine. By the end of the year 2019, the world was hit by a deadly virus outbreak, which resulted in a pandemic called Covid-19. Up until the moment I write this sentence, 1.26 million people have been killed worldwide. To contain the spread of virus, the infected people and those who had contact with Covid-19 patients are being quarantined. I had come in contact with a cousin of mine who was infected and here I am now, in quarantine.

Now, let me tell you what it means to be in quarantine. You spend 14 days all alone in a government quarantine facility or a room in your home. During the period, you are not supposed to step out of the facility; you are not supposed to talk to anyone, not supposed to come in close contact with anyone. You simply sit, lie, sleep or walk up and down in the room, food will be supplied on time and your only means of contact with the rest of the world is the internet and your mobile phone. Currently, I am quarantined in my own room in the comfort of my home. I have special plates and glasses. Usually, I place my plate out of my door for my wife to supply food, without coming in contact with me. She is taking good care of me. Apart from the delicious food, she also prepares a special Ayurvedic medicine with several herbs like Tulsi, ginger, pepper... etc as its ingredients. It is supposed to boost my immunity to fight the virus, in case I have been infected. Let me tell you frankly, it is quite hot and spicy, yet it tastes a lot of love and care.

Though being in quarantine physically cuts you off from the rest of the world, on its flip-side, you get a royal treatment. With a whole room all to myself, a loving wife who supplies food and medication without any delay, and my parents and brothers ensuring that I get to eat only protein-rich food, often, I feel like a king. Natural, right? However, solitude is not that great, right? What is your say? Normally, I would prefer playing with my son, having good time with my wife, working, hanging out with friends or having chit-chat with my family members. But, given the situation, I have two options before me:

1) Either make myself more miserable by cursing the situation, or

2) Make use of the situation

I could make myself more miserable, sitting depressed and curing the situation the whole day. I could curse my cousin with whom I had come in contact, I could curse the health department or I could curse the WHO or the virus... The list would go long. If I make myself more miserable, who stands to lose? Myself. No one else would lose a thing by making myself a cry-baby.

I chose the second one. I chose to make most of the situation. I chose to turn the situation around to benefit me. I use this opportunity to catch up with my friends and relatives, calling them on phone and sharing pleasantries with each other. Besides, I am trying to complete the remaining chapters of my book as I am currently writing this chapter that you are reading now. Furthermore, I set up a mini-studio in my room to record lectures for my next online course. I have no webcam, so I am using my phone to record the lectures. Initially, there was a trouble with the lighting and it was solved when I pulled up the window-curtains. Now I have a luxury of time to watch videos on YouTube, surf on the internet and sleep like a log.

The most mysterious thing in the world is what will happen to you in the next moment. Life is, basically, unpredictable. We plan something, while life plans something else for us. In the crossroads of life, the way forward is to accept it, adapt to it and keep moving with a smile on your face.

Now, imagine that black colour represents sadness, stress, anxiety, depression and such negative states of mind while the white colour represents joy, freedom, hope, happiness and such positive emotions. Now, close your eyes, take a deep breath and try to imagine objects in white colour. It could be anything. Take 30 seconds to do this before you continue reading further.

Sky, paper, nails, light. You might have seen a lot of objects in white colour. Maybe 100 or more. Now close your eyes one more time. Try to see objects in black colour. Take your time before reading further.

Probably, you would find only one or two objects in black. What is happening here? You find what you are looking for. If you look for happiness, you find it. If you look for sadness, you find it too.

> "Keep your face to the sunshine and you cannot see a shadow."
>
> \- Helen Keller

If you look for positive energy, you get it. If you look for negative energy, you get it. If you look for depression, you have it. If you look for happiness, you have it. Life is like that. Look for good, and you will get the best.

> "You see what you seek."
>
> - Muneer Amayoor

16 HUMILIATION, A BLESSING IN DISGUISE

Imagine this situation. In fact, I want you to actually visualise this situation. Imagine, you have been invited as a guest to an institution. When you arrive, you are welcomed with all the honours that are usually bestowed upon a guest. Visualise. All the speakers who spoke before you had been praising you to the sky. And when you finally walk towards the podium, the crowd is cheering for you. Visualise yourself in the situation. But, once you start your speech, everything turns for the worst. Without listening to what you are saying, you are instantly ridiculed by the audience, for your voice, pronunciation and your style of speech. The whole audience erupts and starts booing at you. They hurl humiliating rude comments at you and you feel that you just want to melt away in a second.

I hope you visualised yourself in this situation. Now, what if it happened for real? Well, it did. This is exactly what I experienced when I was once invited as a chief guest to an English Medium school. It was when I was just starting my speaking career. Frankly speaking, I did not have an extensive experience at the time. I had taken great effort to prepare for the talk which was rehearsed multiple times the night before. But I was barely into my third sentence when the audience started booing at me. Can you believe that? They did not know what I was going to talk about, they did not know what I had in my plan and yet my first two sentences were enough for them to declare me worthless. They judged me for my voice, my pronunciation and my speaking style.

After somehow managing to speak for around five minutes, I quickly escaped from there. I was hurt. I was humiliated like never before or after. It was painful, and I will never forget that day in my life.

On that night, I could not sleep. I lay on my back for some time, I lay flat on my stomach for some time. I lay on my left then on my right for some time. But, sleep did not come. The feeling of humiliation still continued to hurt me, it made me angry at times. Sometimes, I hated myself for my voice and pronunciation. Yet, I did not give up; I did not concede my defeat. On that night, I took a strong resolve, no matter what happens, my next goal is to be a truly confident English speaker. I took it as a challenge.

Do you know what I do now? Apart from working as a programme producer and presenter at All India Radio, on Udemy, now I teach students from all over the world. To be precise, I teach students from 117 different countries. Can you guess the medium of instruction? English!

> "One word of Humiliation can lead you to a whole world of success."
>
> –SatyaDeep Trivedi

When was the last time you felt humiliated, and how did you respond? If you develop the right mindset, being humiliated can be a great blessing in disguise. Take it as an opportunity to ignite yourself and prove others wrong.

> "Turn the humiliation to a trigger for rejuvenation."
>
> - Muneer Amayoor

17 A SPACE OF ONE'S OWN

It took me three attempts to get through the PG entrance test. In the third attempt, when I just managed to get through, I thought, "Why should I stop here? Why can't I dream higher?" I thought, I could try cracking UGC NET, which would qualify me to be a University Professor. UGC test is one of the hardest tests in India to crack. However, my experience with the preparation for the entrance test had taught me that if I try hard enough, I could crack it too. Then, why not try?

Since I was damn serious about it, I thought I should have a special place to do my preparation. And I did find a suitable place for me. It was not home, nor at the college. 32 kilo meters away from my home, in the central library of the University of Calicut, I found a promising base for my studies. Every day, I would start off with my books and lunch-box to the university library. As I did not have a library membership, I had to pay ₹10 to use the library facilities. The same routine was continued for next couple of months. Apart from providing books and e-resources for my preparation, the

University Library offered a truly academic environment. Around me, here and there could be found students, M.Phil/PhD scholars and Indian Civil Service aspirants with their heads buried in books. It was the perfect place.

Thomas Alwa Edison, the scientist with so many inventions to his credit, had Menlo Park where he conducted his experiments. He felt most creative inside Menlo Park and many of his inventions were made right there. For me, the Central Library of the University of Calicut was what Menlo Park was for Edison. The surroundings inspired me to learn more and dig more into the books. After a few months, the result was published. I had passed the test with flying colours.

A place which puts you to the right mood, an area which can put you in the top gear and lets your thoughts flow, uninterrupted. Such a place can help you to increase your productivity, tenfold. It can be a special room in your house, a rented space, a corner in the nearby park, or even a tree hut.

> "Concentrate all your thoughts upon the work at hand. The sun's rays do not burn until brought to a focus."
>
> \- Alexander Graham Bell

Like Virginia Woolf's "A Room of One's Own", let's call it "A Space of My Own". If you can designate or make "A Space of My Own" for you to do your most passionate works, it could help you harvest more yield. As you enter this zone, your subconscious mind will automatically shift to its top gear and increase your efficiency many fold. Do you have such a space? If not, make or find one.

"Acknowledge your environmental sensitivity and design a perfect workstation for you."
- Muneer Amayoor

18 DISSECT YOUR CHALLENGES

Life throws at us, challenge after challenge, some of us succeed in facing them while some others miserably fail. Why some people seem to be more equipped to face challenges while some others appear to be less equipped?

Let me tell you a story from the great Mahabharata. One night, the two celebrated brothers, Krishna and Balarama, were travelling through a dreaded forest. When they got exhausted, they decided to stop walking to catch some sleep. Since the forest was notorious for many carnivorous animals and monsters, it was not safe to sleep unguarded. The brothers come up with a solution, it was decided that they would take turns sleeping; while one of them sleeps, the other one would keep watch. First, it was Krishna's turn to sleep. Balarama was tasked with guarding him from any harm. At midnight, out of nowhere, a frightening monster appeared and it roared at Balarama. Poor Balarama was frightened. However, he did not make any noise since Krishna was fast asleep. When the monster noted that Balarama was frightened by him, the monster grew double in size and roared for a second time. Balarama was apparently shaking with fear. With renewed confidence, the monster again grew double in size. Within a short time, the monster became as huge as a mountain. Frightened, Balarama yelled, "Krishna, Krishna" and passed out. There he was lying unconscious right next to Krishna. When Krishna woke up, he found Balarama lying unconscious and thought he was actually asleep and it was his turn to guard. He stood up on his feet and looked around. He did not notice the monster though. The monster roared at Krishna. Without a sign of fear on his face, Krishna looked straight into the monster's eyes and asked, "Who are you?" In an instant, the monster shrank half in size. "What do you want?", Krishna asked again. Again, the monster shrank half in size. Seeing Krishna's courage and valour, gradually, the monster began to shrink more and in no time, it became so small that Krishna could easily hold it in his palm. He picked the little monster in his hand and put it in his pocket.

In the morning, when Balarama woke up, he still had the fear on his face and recounted the previous night's encounter with the monster. He told Krishna that they were super lucky that they made it to the dawn without getting harmed by the monster. Krishna smiled, and took out the monster from his pocket, "Balarama, are you talking about this monster?"

In the face of challenges, some people get instantly frightened and freeze. As a result, the challenge would grow bigger and bigger. On the other hand, a few other people look straight at the challenge and device a way out. They ask themselves the following questions.

1. What is the challenge I am faced with?

2. What caused the challenge to rise?

3. What is the way out?

4. Who can help?

5. What resources would I need to face the challenge?

6. What would be the possible roadblocks on the way?

7. What skills do I have to acquire in order to tackle the situation?

8. What is the first and immediate step I must take?

"All problems become smaller when you confront them instead of dodging them."
- William F. Halsey

Once you are ready to address the challenge at hand, you can feel the difficulties melting down like an ice cube in a warm environment.

> **"Dissect the challenge until it shrinks to fit your palm."**
> **- Muneer Amayoor**

19 THE TEN SECONDS

"I feel extra-confident for tomorrow's test. I've learned every module, cover to cover.", the night before the Biology exam, while having dinner with the family, I announced with a great deal of confidence. It was a busy night, I should say. I had a tough time studying all those Biological terms. Anyway, I was able hit my bed with immense confidence.

The bell rang; I was all set to take the test. First, the answer sheets were provided and I filled in the details, my name, subject, class and everything. In the column to write the name of the subject, in neat capital letters I wrote, "BIOLOGY". When the second bell rang, the invigilator distributed the question papers. To my complete astonishment, on the top of the question paper it read, "Mathematics". Apparently, the teacher had distributed the wrong question paper. I turned to my friend sitting at the other end of the bench, and in a hushed voice, I said, "Hey see this, I got the wrong question paper." He smiled and said, "No, Muneer. Today, it's Mathematics test. Didn't you check our timetable?"

My heart skipped a few beats. Confidence gave way for terror.

Did you ever have such an experience? Missing an appointment date with an important client, carrying the wrong document to the office, or going for a marriage on a wrong date? I can see why you are smiling.

What is the best way not to repeat such mistakes? One word-reconfirm – that is the only way. Do not blindly believe your memory. By its very nature, it is designed to fail at times, but, the reality will not change. Before you start with any major work, pose for a while, go through your schedule and reconfirm your priorities. Take a moment to look at your diary before you start your car to meet the client you have an appointment with. Look at the exam time table once again on the eve of the exam. Ensure, you carry the right documents before going for the meeting. Ensure that you have copied the right files needed for your presentation. You will require only less than ten seconds to do these. However, you may incur huge loss of time, money, health and effort if you do not develop this habit. Just ten seconds. That's all it takes to avoid life-long regrets.

"Trust, but verify."

– Ronald Regan

Trust your memory, but do not blindly believe it. Take actions to verify it. You shall reap its benefits.

> "A look at the checklist on time saves a thousand regrets later."
>
> \- Muneer Amayoor

20 ADAPT OR PERISH

A sea-food restaurant on the beach road overlooking the sea. A restaurant, easily accessible to the people visiting the beach, surfers, and the community in the area. A restaurant that serves exclusively sea food. Jim and his friend, Richard started the restaurant business with great hope. The starting was fantastic. They got customers. However, the food items were costly. In the initial days, they got customers from many areas. Later, there was a decline in the number of customers. They supplied the best food. The service was also the best. Still, the number of customers and everyday income was on a steady decline. In a few months, the team was losing money. Still, Jim and Richard kept on going thinking that some miracle would happen, and they would be able to turn things around. When they could not get the money even to pay the employees, they took loan and continued, hoping that one day it would be okay. It was too late by the time they realised that the prices that they had set will not work in that area. The pricing was suitable for a bigger city with a large population, but not for the current city. Besides, most of the customers were tourists visiting and they were only seasonal customers. Soon, they incurred a huge debt and they could not keep running the business anymore. Inevitably, they were forced to shut down the business.

Sometimes, we may make wrong decisions. It is important to correct the path at the earliest. Slow and steady changes are difficult to identify. Here in this restaurant, what happened was they could not see where the business was headed as the decline in the number of customers was slow and steady. If the duo had kept a vigil eye on the business, they could have been able to identify the flaw in their business model on time and they could have taken solid actions to keep the business afloat. If they had identified it earlier, they would have stood a chance to change the dishes from only sea food to a complete non-vegetarian restaurant. They could have changed the pricing pattern to attract more customers. What they lacked was a vigil eye to spot slow but steady developments and the courage to correct their own path.

If you put two frogs into two different pots with water in them and heat them up, one quickly, and the other one slowly, do you know what would happen? The frog in the pot which was heated quickly will jump out and make its escape. The other frog, on the other hand, will adjust its body temperature with respect to the increasing temperature of the water. At some point, the water would become too hot, beyond which the frog cannot survive. By that time, the frog would have lost all its energy in its attempt to adjust its own body temperature. Then it would have no option left, but to die in that boiling water.

> "If you fail, never give up because FAIL means, First Attempt In Learning. End is not the end, in fact END means, Effort Never Dies. If you get No as an answer, remember NO means, Next Opportunity."
>
> – Dr.A.P.J.Abdul Kalam

Are you a keen observer? Observe your surroundings well to sense the changes, and to adapt yourself accordingly. Or, be prepared to perish like the ill-fated frog in the pot.

> "An intelligent miner knows when to stop digging. You should know when to stop investing time and money on something."
>
> - Muneer Amayoor

21 UNBLOCK THE WAY

"What is happening with our daughter? Her math-teacher just called me, complaining about her poor performance."

"I don't know what to do about it. Our daughter is just so weak in mathematics."

"Yes, she is excellent in every other subject. But..."

"Even the home-tuition is not helping her."

"Exactly, I thought, she would improve after starting this home-tuition....But...."

"Maybe, she is like that, she is just so weak in math"

"Hmm.. Maybe it's like that. What to do?"

Sana's parents thought that it was only a private conversation between them. But, the five-year old overheard the whole conversation from her study room. Actually, Sana was a smart student, though she found Mathematics a bit difficult to learn. Her concerned parents arranged a home tuition for her. Every day, a teacher came to her home, and taught her to add and subtract numbers. But, it did not help her much. She was already deeply worried about her trouble with Maths and then she heard her parents' conversation. Parents' words shot through her heart like a bullet. It left her shattered and made Mathematics appear like a hard nut she could never crack.

Can you guess, what happened to little Sana afterwards? She got promoted to the second grade, then to the third, then to the fourth and so on and so forth. Besides, she excelled in every field. Apart from excelling in her curricular subjects, she also made it to the school choir team as a leading singer, representing the school in several competitions and winning trophies for the school. Her father hired a carpenter to make a special showcase to display the awards and trophies his daughter had bagged. Yet, her achievements had a flip-side. Despite all her achievements, maths continued to be a nightmare for her. For her, every math test was a battleground she was destined to lose. "I did everything I can. But, I don't know why, I cannot learn this subject. I hate it." She cursed at times.

Over the years, dozens of teachers taught her Maths and dozens of teachers tutored her. Yet, little help did she get. When she reached the ninth grade, however, her class teacher, Sushama noticed Sana, who scored best marks in every subject, but failed in Mathematics. Once, the teacher noticed Sana sitting alone on a bench in a corner of the class, trying hard to hold her tears back. The teacher, instantly knew, what was going on. The teacher took hold of Sana's hand and led her to the teacher' cabin. "Sit here, my dear." said the teacher in a compassionate voice, "Please make yourself comfortable". Sushama's tender-hearted behaviour struck a chord with Sana and for the next one and half hours, they kept on talking. Sana poured her heart out to the teacher who was keenly listening to Sana's childhood stories, she revealed how she had overheard her parents' conversation and how ever since then, she was terrified by Mathematics.

"Oh....dear, you know what? You are what you decide to be. You are not what others think about you, you are not what others say about you. You are what you decide to be. Nothing more, nothing less. Only thing that is holding you back in Mathematics now, is that little thought your parents put in your mind when you were just a little kid. Actually, you can be excellent in math just as in any other subject", the teacher said, patting Sana's shoulders.

Sana smiled, and asked.

"But... teacher, how. . . . how can I improve in Math?"

"It is your thoughts that put you behind. So, it is again your thoughts that can bring you to the front."

"What do you mean, miss?", curious Sana asked.

"You do one thing. Write 'I am very good in Mathematics. I enjoy learning this subject', in a few pieces of paper. Then, paste them on your bed room wall, reading table, kitchen and everywhere you can think of. Paste one of them on your wall in such a way that it would be the first thing you would see when you wake up in the morning. When you read it, visualise yourself solving math problems like a boss. Tell yourself that you are a math-geek. Do this for 4 weeks and come back to me.", Sushama said.

Sana did everything as her teacher instructed. Often, her parents gave a bewildered look, but Sana did not care to explain herself. Except for the fact that her little brother often used to rip it off the wall and she had to paste new pieces every now and then, Sana found no major trouble on her way. With a new-found confidence, she began to attend the math-classes.

After 4 weeks' time, Sana went back to her teacher, Sushama. Her eyes were shining out of joy.

"I have started enjoying the subject now", announced Sana, "I used to see Mathematics as a monster, but now I see it as my friend."

"Wow, that's absolutely wonderful. Now, invest more time for the subject, and do not hesitate to get back to your math teacher if you have any doubt.", teacher encouraged Sana. Her parents' words had left a lasting impression in her mind, now with her teacher's help, Sana was able to reprogramme her mind.

> **"Being what most people think is realistic is only a way of justifying negative thinking. Go for something great."**
>
> **– Dr. Bob Rotella**

What do you think about the future performance of Sana? How well will she perform? Can you guess what shift in her mindset brought this change?

> **"If you feel stuck on something, trace back and re-program your mind."**
>
> **- Muneer Amayoor**

22 MAKE IT SIMPLE

How can you check whether or not you have understood a topic clearly? Can it be done by memorising and verbalising what you have learned? Or by checking if you can reproduce it in writing? Even if you can mechanically parrot or write it 100 times, does it mean that you have, actually, digested the topic? In other words, does being able to reproduce what you have learned, guarantee that you have understood the topic? No. If this happens to be your favourite method of learning, I am sorry to bust your myth. Memorising is simply memorising. For understanding, you have to go an extra mile.

Nobel Prize winning physicist Richard Feynman has proposed a useful technique to check your understanding. First, you learn the topic in your own way. For the purpose, you can use any learning method of your choosing. Secondly, imagine that you are the teacher of a ten-year old kid and explain the topic in such a way that even your student could understand. Thirdly, when you explain the topic, if you notice certain areas where you have difficulty in explaining, simply mark those areas. Re-read and re-learn that area. Again, explain the topic as if you are talking to that ten-year old child. Repeat the same process until you can explain the whole topic to your imaginary student in the simplest way.

If he/she could understand, it means that you have understood it! Once you feel that you are confident to explain it to a kid in the simplest way, then, you can say that you have understood the topic. The key is in being able to explain in the simplest way. If you cannot do that, it means that you have only memorised the idea, not understood it.

> "I don't know what's the matter with people: they don't learn by understanding, they learn by some other way — by rote or something. Their knowledge is so fragile!"
>
> \- Richard Feynman

Next time you try to learn anything related to your studies, business or any other field, make it a point to use Feyman's technique.

> "Simplicity is the key to clear understanding."
>
> \- Muneer Amayoor

23 IDENTIFY THE ROOT CAUSE

Once, a teacher aged 50 years, called me on phone. He sounded completely crestfallen and pessimistic and told me that he was fed up with teaching, and he feels like quitting the job. We talked over the phone for almost 48 minutes. I asked him to tell me five benefits that he was receiving from the job. He listed its monetary, social, spiritual and developmental benefits. Then, I asked him why he was feeling that he was not apt for the job. He revealed that he had used to be a mediocre student when he was studying, which he believed, made him a misfit in the profession. Then, I proceeded to ask about the students, teachers and parents' feedback about his class. He replied that he got favourable feedback from everyone. From the way talked, I could feel that he was actually an excellent teacher, but something bothered him. I could not pinpoint what was actually bothering him. Sensing the need for more clarity in his issue, I asked him if he would prefer an appointment for a direct talk. He said yes and the date and time were fixed.

After a detailed analysis of his past and history at the workplace, I could sense that the actual reason for his dislike for his job, was not because he hated the job as such, nor was it because he felt that, he was a misfit in the teaching profession. I could pinpoint his negative attitude towards his profession to an unpleasant experience he once had, a ten-year old experience.

To cut the long story short, the teacher used to be quite friendly with one of his lady colleagues. The lady colleague in question used to call him and he did not object to it as he did not give any romantic shade to the relationship. But, not the lady. She thought of the relationship as a purely romantic one though. The teacher was completely unaware of it. Later, the teacher's wife found out about the relation and she could sense what was going on. The issue quickly escalated into a fight and it caused a rift between the couple.

As the teacher's wife could understand what was actually going on, at the time, it did not cause any major trouble. Besides, the very next day, the teacher did just what was right to do. He talked with the lady colleague, telling her what happened and blamed her for taking their relationship to the next level causing rift between himself and his wife. He convinced her not call him again and not to pursue any romantic relationship with him. The colleague understood him well, repented and no longer bothered him. It was supposed to be the end of the story. But it did not. Ten years after the issue, it was still haunting him. Though both the colleagues kept away from each other, the teacher's wife often felt paranoid that the old relation may come back and rob him away. She felt insecure and he knew about that. Besides, the same old colleague still worked in the same school where he worked.

Now, can you guess why the teacher wanted to quit his job as a teacher? As he thinks, did he really hate teaching profession? Did he really feel that he was a misfit in the field? No! He may have felt like quitting his job. But, contrary to what he thought, not because he hated teaching as such. Whereas, he felt that his work and his workplace are potential threats to his marital relationship which he valued more than anything. His own mind was cheating him, making him think that he is a misfit in the profession.

How can he overcome this issue now? He cannot erase his memories, but he can stop his memories from hurting him and making him afraid. For that, he needs to treat the root cause for his problem, which is attitude towards his workplace and his experience with the colleague that almost cost him his marriage. He does not have to quit his job, nor does he not have to hate his job. He only has to do three things:

1) Accept the fact that he does not actually hate his job.

2) Accept that the root cause for his problem is his attitude towards his workplace and he needs to change it.

3) To change his attitude towards his workplace, he needs to ask for his wife's forgiveness and forgive her back, along with forgiving his colleague.

Fortunately, I was able to relieve him by changing his attitude and making him accept the root cause for his trouble through a hypnotic session. I also convinced his wife to fully forgive her husband and let go the unpleasant memory.

Sometimes, it happens to everyone. Our minds trick us into attributing our issue to some wrong reasons and we go about treating these wrong reasons to solve our issue. It will not work. The primary step to solve any issue is to identify the root cause. The root cause may or may not have a history behind it. It may be haunting memories from your past-from childhood, college days or even recent past.

"Maybe you are searching among the branches,
for what only appears in the roots."

– Rumi

Now, look back at your past. Is there any wound yet to be healed? If yes, bring yourself to forgive the person who caused the wound. In time, you will experience a miraculous change both in your physical and mental health. All the roadblocks will disappear and peace will fill your mind.

"Identifying the root cause is the first step to heal your wounds."

- Muneer Amayoor

24 DRESS TO WIN HEARTS

I remember a training programme I had attended. After the inaugural ceremony and such formalities, the Resource Person was introduced. The formal session was a boring ordeal to sit through and it was with much anticipation we were waiting for the session handled by the Resource Person. After almost half an hour or so, the much awaited session was about to start and the RP presented himself on the floor. The first impression that he made on me, in particular, and the whole audience, in general, was not quite impressive. With his coat and suite that matched the occasion, he might have hoped to make an immediate impact on the audience. But all that I remember about the session now is his odd choice of necktie. To his navy-blue suite, for some strange reasons, he chose to wear a deep yellow necktie with red dots on it. It made a striking contrast that made his appearance eye-catchy. But, sadly, for the wrong reason. In the first few minutes of his lecture, I could not help wondering all the possible reasons for his odd choice. However, thanks to that choice he had made, it is only that tie, I still remember from the session. What you wear does have a huge psychological impact on the people you meet. It is sad that the appearance can be deceptive and yet it is so important. Like it or not, we must accept the fact that, we humans are biologically wired and programmed to make quick judgments.

Now, coming to you, how many dresses do you have? Can you count them? I know why you are smiling now, you have literally a lot of them, right? Anyway, if you do not pay much attention to what you wear, you might want to read this chapter carefully. It is true that appearance can be deceptive. Yet, how you groom yourself and how you present yourself do have a psychological impact on yourself and those around you. That simply means, you cannot wear any kind of dress to anywhere.The kind of dress that you wear to the office must be something plain and yet it should command respect from others. It would look odd if you wear the same dress to a party. You would look ridiculously funny if you go jogging wearing your office-wear. Similarly, what if you wear your Yoga Pants to an interview? If you are going to speak at a conference, you ought to dress in a certain way that gives you great confidence. Attending a funeral ceremony wearing an extravagant party-wear would earn you enemies.

What you wear matters. This is not to suggest that you must wear only expensive dresses. Wear anything that suits to your taste as long as it suits the occasion. The logic must be applied to your inner wears as well. Wait before giving me that look! You might ask, "Inner wears? Seriously? Who sees my inner wears?" Well, nobody sees them, sure, but you know what you wear underneath, right? As long as you know what you wear, it will affect your confidence level.

From inner wears to blazers, everything counts. Your foot wear is probably the garment that people would subconsciously look at. Make sure that your shoes are clean and polished. Whatever you wear, find time to iron your clothes and get set to go. Neat and tidy, simple and beautiful – such a dressing style will help you appear more approachable, which will, in turn, help you forge quick connections with the people you meet. Simplicity easily wins hearts.

> **"You never get a second chance to make a first impression."**
>
> **– Will Rogers**

Prophet Muhammed told: "Verily, The God is handsome, and he loves beauty." Imagine that the world is a theatre. As an actor on this stage, present yourself in the best costume possible. Now, get ready to go with the most suitable outfit and make the best impact on the people! Your self-image is at stake here!

> "Be groomed or be doomed."
>
> - Muneer Amayoor

25 FIND YOUR BALANCE

The first to arrive in the office and the last to leave, Ratheesh is a hard-working professional. On a typical day in the office he can be found with a pile of files on his desk, painstakingly going through them, looking for errors and correcting them as he goes. Spinning a pencil around his fingers, his eyes would tirelessly work thoroughly scrutinising each and every word in the file. If he ever lifts his eyes to face someone, his bulging eyes could be seen through his bottle glasses. Often, it looks like his eyeballs are about to drop. Perfectionism is key-motto. He makes sure that everything is done in the super perfect way. If he is asked to make a draft note, he will first write it on a piece of paper, search for the most suitable words on Google, and verify the grammar countless times. Then, he will type it in the computer. The formatting will be re-adjusted several times to ensure the best look. After taking the print-out, he will proof read, edit, retype and reprint.

What do you think about Ratheesh? If the manager assigns him with any task, the manager needs not worry about any errors. Precisely for this reason, whenever there is a crucial document to be made, the manager entrusts Ratheesh with the task. But, it has a flip side. When other staff members leave the office, their table will be usually empty. On Ratheesh's table on the other hand, there will be a huge pile of files all the time. He could not even remember the last time he finished his daily target on time. He never does. When others work on 9 to 5 work shift, Ratheesh starts his work as early as 8 AM and his work would go as long as 7'O clock in the late evening. He has a separate pair of keys for the office.

Despite his complete dedication and perfectionism, he was not happy with his work. More seriously, he found his life dull and boring. He felt that he spent most of his time, to be more precise, around 12 hours a day, working like a machine in his office. All at the cost of spending quality time with his wife and children. It has been 6 months since he promised his wife to take her and children out for a picnic. So far, he could not get around to it. Even during weekends, he tried to finish his pending works. Yet, at the workplace, he was not given the respect he deserved. Never did he receive any word of recognition from his colleagues or superiors. They taunted him calling "Mr. Perfectionist" or "nerdy nut".

"If you look for perfection, you'll never be content."

- Leo Tolstoy

All work and no play made Ratheesh a dull boy! His efforts go underappreciated, and his family life is at stake. How would you feel if you were in his place? What do you think, he should do?

"Perfectionists never finish anything, and even if they finish, satisfaction will be a distant dream."

- Muneer Amayoor

26 MASTER YOUR DEVICES

One day, I was having dinner with my family. Usually, we dine together, which surely strengthens our love and bonds. Apart from the sheer joy it provides, family dinner comes with an ideal time to teach your little ones about sharing food with each other. Suddenly, my mobile phone started to ring, I had left it in my room. "Hey, your phone is ringing." said my wife.

"I know, let it ring for the time being. I will call back after the food." I replied.

The question is, do you control your devices, or do they control you? Do you have the urge to check out your social media accounts every now and then? Or do you have the urge to reply to the messages you receive, irrespective of your time? Is your quality time with your family or friends frequently punctuated with phone calls you receive? Well, if your answer is "yes", I am sorry to tell you that you are being controlled by your devices.

Mobile devices and other gadgets are supposed to make your life easier and faster so that you can save your time to productively engage in things that matter the most. They are supposed to be your aides. Sadly, many of us end up being slave to our aides. What a tragic twist! Modern life has come to the point that you can manage your life, only if you know how to manage your devices. In the meantime, we must acknowledge the fact that, the computers and mobile devices act like double-edged swords. On the one hand, they can help you in connecting with people who are far away from you. On the other hand, what is the point of being connected with people who are away while you fail to truly connect with the person sitting next to you? Your devices can help you in connecting with your clients or potential customers and thereby further your business interests. At the same time, they can steal your quality time and make you a digital slave. These devices have a way of encroaching into our private life and that has to be stopped at any cost. Imagine you are playing with your kid and suddenly your boss rings you and you decide to attend the call. One moment, you are a loving father, the next moment a respectful subordinate and the next moment, if possible, back to being a caring father again. How awkwardly artificial our relations turn out to be. And what is the worst of them all? The worst development is that it has been normalised and many of us even fail to recognise that our being a digital slave could harm our relations. It is time we found a balance between our life online and life offline.

Even while at work, your devices might keep pressing you to check it out. You may be curious to know how many people have reacted to your new post on your social media accounts, you might feel the urge to respond to the comments and messages you received, and you might be excited to know what your friends are up to. All of these are natural. However, if you can manage that thirst, you can triple your productivity, and get more done in less time. One more thing, all these are relative. For some kinds of work, especially if you are employed as a public relation manager, responding to the online activities will be an essential part of your work. In such cases, a different approach is required-you can respond to the queries and such other online activities in such a way that it does not sneak into your private life.

Now, how can we try finding a perfect balance between our life online and life offline? There are a couple of hacks you can follow. Firstly, assigning only particular time of the day to check your social media accounts would do wonders for you. For example, half an hour after your lunch or half an hour after your workout would be ideal time to allocate for social media.

After all, both these times, you could not be truly effective or productive. However, note that, from a psychological point of view, opening and closing your day with online activities could be counterproductive. Secondly, be realistic about your goal. You can't get rid of your social media addiction on a fine morning. Like any other addiction it could take time. The wise decision would be to gradually cut down on the time you spend online. Thirdly, do not sit idle. Not being engaged in anything could activate the proverbial devil inside you. If you develop some offline hobby, or a passion for something, your free time could be channelized towards them.

Simply put, your goal must be to be your own captain, the ship of your everyday life should follow the course you set, not the course set by your devices.

One hack that does wonders for me, is turning off notifications button. Now, the frequent notifications no longer trigger my urge to check out my devices.

> "It's not enough to be busy, so are the ants.
> The question is, what are we busy about?"
>
> \- Henry David Thoreau

Your devices can be your enemies or your assistants. It depends on who the master is. You? Or your device?

> "Your devices are your aides, do not be the slave to your aides."
>
> \- Muneer Amayoor

27 WHERE IS YOUR KEY?

"Where is it? Neethu, did you see my key?"

Clean shaven and wearing his neatly ironed clothes, Athul was frantically running from his room to his to his sister's room. His mother had placed his tiffin box safely inside his office bag. His sister had ironed his shirt for him. He should have hit the road at least by 9.15 AM to reach his office on time. It is 9.30 now and yet he is running from room to room looking for his bike's key.

"I have my own stuff to keep, I don't know where your key is", screamed his sister while sweeping the courtyard.

"Son, check on the table in the living room. I had seen it there." said his father without even lifting his eyes from the newspaper he was scrutinising.

"Aah, there it is. Mom I am going. I will definitely be late today," announced Athul while hoping onto his bike. In fact, he is late almost every day and the usual culprit, as you guessed already, would be the same every day-the key.

Did you ever have similar experiences? From what I know about my friends and relatives, I guess that many of you can relate to Athul's experience. Do you remember where you have kept your bike/car's key? Do you remember where you have kept your pendrive? Any idea where you have placed the cash receipt from the supermarket? How many times have you bought a new pen because you have lost the one you had been using? Do you ever get hold of that elusive nail-cutter when you really need it? Sometimes, these things are dismissed as silly matters and they end up stealing your valuable time.

You can save your valuable time and reach office/school/college/workplace on time, if you designate a specific place for your "silly" stuff like key, nail-cutter, pendrive and such. I shall tell you about a hack that works well enough for me. Let me admit it, I used to be just like Athul. Later, I made myself a simple and yet beautiful key hanger using my old abandoned belt. A simple DIY hack. Now, thanks to the efforts that have gone into its making and how beautiful it seems to me, I hang my bike's key on the same key-hanger every day. I love seeing it hang there. Another technique you can use is telling yourself where you have kept your stuff. For example, when you place some stuff or documents at certain place, make it point to tell yourself that you have kept it there. If you keep your key on the table, tell yourself "I have placed my key on the table". Say it loud enough so that the idea will be consciously registered in your subconscious mind. You won't forget it again.

> "There is no magic wand that can resolve our problems. The solution rests with our work and discipline. "
>
> - Jose Eduardo dos Santos

Little hacks can sometimes make greater impacts on your life. Develop your own hacks to keep moving faster, smoother and better.

> "Declutter to get better at the art of discipline."
>
> - Muneer Amayoor

28 GOODBYE TO PHOBIA

After a training programme for teenage girls in a school, a girl approached me and said that she had a problem of hospital fear.

"I dread at the thought of hospitals and doctors. I know it's kind of stupid, can you help me, sir?", the girl asked me. By the way, for your information, the fear of hospitals is called Nosocomephobia.

Basically, she was afraid of doctors, nurses, medical equipments and hospitals in general. For this reason, she felt deeply uncomfortable and anxious whenever she visited hospitals when she was sick. I talked to her for a while and soon the root cause for her fear came to light. When she was young, she was hospitalised for some health issues and she had to take painful injections on a regular basis. The painful experience in her young days had left a deep scar in her mind and as a result, every time she thought of doctors or hospitals, she was reminded of the nightmarish hospital experiences she had. However, she did not know what was actually going on. All that she knew was that hospitals terrorised her. I decided to help her and fortunately, it worked out as expected.

I asked her to close her eyes and imagine that she was sitting in a movie theatre. Then I asked her to imagine her drifting into the projector room from her seat.

"Your mind is the projector, use your imagination to visualise everything that I say."

I told her to visualise a closed door on the screen.

"You are now going to open the door. It is a hospital. You can see, doctors and nurses in their white uniforms, casualty section, ICU, operation theatre, labs, scanning rooms and patients. Imagine everything with full details. Now, please enter the hospital, go to the doctor's cabin and talk to him. What a friendly man! He is welcoming you with a friendly smile and by touching you in the most gentle way, he is examining you. In a calm voice, he is telling you that there is nothing much to worry that you have only a seasonal flue. A sense of comfort is spreading in your mind. Look to your left side, don't you see a smiling nurse? She looks like an angel, doesn't she? She is softly giving you a flue-shot. Her fingers feel so soft and you did not even know when it was done."

She listened to my instructions and responded well.

I continued, "Now, take a long and deep breath. Take two more. Now, imagine another door. It's the exit door. Don't you see 'exit' written at the top of the door? Walk towards the door, open it and step out. It's outside the hospital now, a beautiful tree, people walking here and there, crows flying in the sky. You are outside the hospital now"

Then I made a sound, "zzzzzzzzzzzzzzzzzz zzzzzzzzzzzzz!" and told her to reverse all the scenes superfast when I make the same sound next time. I told, it was like the rewinding-button on a video player. Then I made the zzzzzzzzzzzzzzzzzzzzzzzzzzzzz-sound. She completed the reversing all the scenes in about 30 seconds.

If you lost the track of the story line, let me remind you, now she is standing in front of the door, just like the beginning of the scene.

"Now, let's watch another movie. A different version of the same movie. Open the door in front you and it's a hospital inside. But it's different. It's a colourful hospital from a Disney cartoon. Colourfully painted hospital with clouds passing over it. Imagine that everything looks like a cartoon, a plumy doctor, nurses who look like fairies and patients who look funny, a funny hospital for a funny cartoon”

Again, I made zzzzzzzzzzzzzzzzzzzzzzzzzzzz-sound, and the movie was reversed in about thirty seconds. One more time, I took her to the same cartoon-like hospital by instructing as follows;

“Open the door and it’s the same cartoon-like hospital again. Same hospital with the same cartoon-like doctors, nurses and funny patients. Yet, there is a big twist this time. Imagine a funny background music to the whole scene. Imagine that funny song from the *Madagascar,* ‘I like to move it, move it, you like to move move it.’ Imagine the doctors dancing to the funny tone, the patients going crazy with their moves and the fairy nurses dancing with the syringes in their hand. Imagine that scene, doctors, nurses, patients and everyone dancing in a Disney-like hospital. A funny hospital”

Again, I said, “zzzzzzzzzzzzzzzzzzzzzzzzzz”. She could see herself standing in front of the first door.

Then I told her to drift back from the projector room to the movie screen and merge her real self with the character on the screen. In a magical hypnotic moment, the character and the mindset of the girl on the screen is transferred to her real self. Then I asked her to drift back to the theatre seat.

"1..2..3..eyes open", I enquired what she felt like after the session.

"I never thought, hospitals can be such a funny place, ha ha", she replied.

Here, I used a variation of NLP technique proposed by Richard Bandler and a hypnotic technique by Freddy Jacquin. Through the session, the girl was able to reprogramme her mind with new images and with the new images came the new attitude. If you have any illogical fear about something, like the girl, it could be because of some negative visual images in your mind about the object of fear. By replacing the image in your mind, you could say goodbye to phobia.

> "Why be your real self when you can be something really worthwhile?"
>
> - Richard Bandler.

What is that image, which makes you feel uncomfortable? Are you ready to replace it by uploading a new cheerful image to your mind? Why wait? Do it now!

"Change the image inside your mind to change what you see outside."

- Muneer Amayoor

29 INVEST ON TECH

Do you own a good smartphone? If not, it is high time you bought one. Yes, good quality smartphone is no longer a dismissible luxury; it is a necessity of our time. It is "a need", not just "a want".

To connect with friends and relatives, to connect with the customers, to do business, to read books, to calculate, to relax, to watch movies, to listen to songs and what not. Nowadays, smartphones function much like a personal assistant. To say "No" to the benefits the AI in the form of smartphones provide is the height of stupidity. The ground beneath our feet has changed and we must change with it. Adopt and adapt. Or risk being an old stick in the mud lagging far behind everyone else. This is noone to suggest that you have to buy the most expensive or the most advanced one. Do your research and buy one that suits best to your needs as well as your budget.

I had a friend, who was suspicious about buying a good smartphone. However, once he knew how it can help him in his business, he dug into his savings to buy a smartphone that suited his business needs. This is called adapting. Meantime, I had another friend, who would upgrade his phone every now and then, sometimes twice a year. He was just a student at that time, his motto was owning the smartest one all the time. With every major new model with more features being unveiled, he would rush into the mobile store to sell his old one and buy the latest model instead. In fact, the urge to own the most technologically advanced phone is not "a need", but a "mere want". Draw a perfect line and find a perfect balancing between your "need" and "want".

Most importantly, note that smartphones are meant to be your personal assistants. They should fuel your growth, not doom. Be wise when you use them.

> **"The tech world is not a new phenomenon; it's a new era."**
>
> **- Boots Riley**

Adapt to the new world, invest in technology. Remember, those who adapt the best and fastest have the best chance of survival and growth.

"If owning a new equipment would make your life better, own it. If that new equipment will steal your time, say 'No' to it."

- Muneer Amayoor

30 WHAT ARE YOU?

What do you do to make a living? You may be a coolie, a carpenter, a mason, a teacher, a driver, a sales executive, a call centre executive, a receptionist or whatever you are. But is that all you are? Are you just a mason and nothing else? Is it right to reduce your identity only to your profession?

As a driver, a person will take passengers from point A to B. Is it right to say that, that is all he does-transporting people? No. On the way, he might pick up a conversation with his passengers and even give them greater clarity on their own life. On the way from point A to B, he might cheer up his passengers with his interesting talks. When he is with his friends, he may be inspiring them with his words. Maybe, it is common that his friends and relatives use to contact him for advice when they are faced with some trouble. Along with transporting people, he might also be a valuable trouble shooter for those around him.

If that is the case, is he to be treated merely as a driver. Please do not get me wrong, every job has its own dignity. Is it right to completely reduce his identity into just a man who takes people from place to place? No. He is a person who inspires hundreds of people, many of them happen to be complete strangers who hire his service and he gives them the clarity and the advice they were in need of. He is a clarity giver, he is an advisor, he is an inspiring man and with his cheerful words, he makes many people's day. Even he may not know this.

Nobody is to be defined only in terms of his/her profession. And most importantly, nobody should reduce himself or herself into just his/her profession. Profession is just what one does to put bread on the plate. If the driver we mentioned, happens to identify him only as a driver, he will not be able to expand his horizon and thereby help thousands of people around him. He may be a driver by the profession, but by his passion, he is a cheerful speaker who can help others see through their own lives.

> "The future belongs to those who believe in the beauty of their dreams."
>
> – Eleanor Roosevelt

Dear friend, I am not asking intrusive questions about your profession. I am more concerned about your passion. You have to earn bread and butter for your family. Find dignity in whatever job you do and do it without any shame or hesitation. At the same time, never say 'No' to your passion.

Pursuing you passion is what would give meaning to your life. How can you identify your passion? To find it, ask yourself the following questions:

- What are the areas I am most interested in?
- What kind of problems have I solved for myself and others?
- What motivates me the most?
- What kind of books/videos/talks/persons motivate me the most?

If you ask these questions to yourself, you will definitely be able to identify where you passion lies. Once identifying it, water and nurture it in every possible way you can. Remember, you are not your profession; you are what you do passionately.

> "If your passion meets profitability, then make it your profession"
>
> \- Muneer Amayoor

31 ACTIVATE THE IMAGINAL CELLS

Do you know how a butterfly is born? When the caterpillar sleeps inside the cocoon, a lot of magical things take place. Inside the cocoon is the chrysalis. Chrysalis is a mix of worm cells and imaginal cells.

The imaignal celles make a great metaphor for the way the champions are born. Let me explain. Imaginal cells are the ones responsible for the metamorphosis, the magical process by which the caterpillars turn into beautiful butterflies. It is "imaginal cells" that help the caterpillar start to develop the new shape of a butterfly.The caterpillar is a worm, very different from a butterfly. Imaginal cells make the magical transformation possible. Initially, each of the imaginal cells operates as a single-cell organism – entirely independent of one another. At the same time, the worm cells will start fighting against the imaginal cells. Soon, the cocoon turns into a battle-field where imaginal cells and worm cells lock horns. In the ensuing fight, if the worm cells win, the metamorphosis will not take place, the caterpillar will remain a worm. However, the imaginal cells never fight to lose. The more imaginal cells are produced, the stronger the opposition will become. However, the imaginal cells perform the magic. They multiply themselves and make bonds with one another, forming clusters that will wage a war against the worm cells. In this way, through a collective effort, the imaginal cells overcome the number of worm cells and beat them to the ground. It is the start of the magical transformation which, literally, gives wings to the caterpillar.

The same kind of war takes place inside each one of us. Inside us also are those metaphoric worm cells and imaginal cells. If you, as a person, have the quality of the imaginal cells, you will be able to defeat the worm cells and emerge as a butterfly in your life. However, easier said than done. It takes a great deal of determination, courage, dedication, wisdom, and faith to awaken the imaginal cells within you.

There are also 'imaginal personalities' around us. They fight against the social evils, and in spite of all the challenges, emerge as champions. Let me introduce you to one such personality I admire a lot. Ubais Sainulabdeen, is a well known name among the human right activists in India. Hailing from Trivandrum, Kerala, he has set an example for all of us to follow.

He was born to a business family. They made beautiful leather bags and sold it all around the country. As part of his business, he used to travel to different parts of India. During such trips, he had made it a hobby to visit the nearby tourist hubs. When he was only 20 years old, as a part of the business, he happened to travel to a remote place in Tamil Nadu. There, he came across some people who were locked behind an iron fence. When he asked to the villagers, he came to know that they were refugees. He wanted to give food for them. Ubais went to a nearby shop and bought bread packets for them. He reached the camp with bread packets in his hand, and started distributing them among the refugees who extended their hand out through the fence. As the refugees rushed for food, one girl fell down on the iron fence while extending her hand for the bread packet. Her head injured and it started to bleed. Seeing this, the security personnel came and beat Ubais. He fell down unconscious. When he got his consciousness back while in a hospital, he took two decisions. He wanted to see the security personnel who beat him and wanted to know, what crime he had done, to deserve such a brutal punishment. Secondly, he wanted to see the little girl who was injured.

With the support of the villagers and the local leaders, he bought a lot more bread packets and went straight to the camp. This time, the security personnel did not interrupt him. The incident had made headlines in major local newspapers. He and his team members distributed the bread packets without being interrupted by anyone. When he asked the mother of the little girl to show her, she refused at first. Anyway, he managed to see her later. When he returned from the camp, he was a new person. This incident was the starting point of the metamorphosis that turned him into a human rights activist.

Now, Ubais is an active campaigner who campaigns for refugee rehabilitation, human rights protection and so much more. When a heavy flood once hit Tamil Nadu and Kerala, he was there in the forefront of the flood mitigation programmes. He is the founder of Ubais Sainulabdeen Peace Foundation which is the driving force behind several human rights campaigns in South India.

Once he told me that, “Jai Jagad” is his motto. It means “May the world win.” He underlines that humans are equal irrespective of their caste, ethnicity, creed, religion, sex, and financial conditions. He divides his revenue from his business into three. One third is for him to support himself and his family, another one third is earmarked for the welfare of his relatives and the last portion is earmarked to support the other struggling people around him. It was not an easy going for him. Once, when he was immensely engaged in his activism, he could not pay amble attention to his business and the business collapsed. He was bankrupt for some time. At that time, the "imaginal cells" inside him awakened and defeated the worm cells. He brought his business back to its feet and it allowed him to raise more fund to support his campaigns. Once, he happened to share his philosophy of life which goes like this: To live a happy life, make the lives of people around you happier. What a great philosophy to follow!

> "What counts is not necessarily the size of the dog in the fight – it's the size of the fight in the dog."
>
> – General Dwight D. Eisenhower

Now tell me, do you have enough strength and determination to help the imaginal cells within you to win the crucial war against the invading worm cells? If not, ask yourself, what are the five immediate things you can do to strengthen the imaginal cells within you.

> "Activate the imaginal cells within you to transform yourself into a beautiful butterfly."
>
> - Muneer Amayoor

32 FACE YOUR FEAR

Let me make a frank revelation about myself. Since you know me as a Personal Growth Architect, and a radio presenter whose passion is talking to people, you might find it hard to believe. Believe it or not, when I was a teenager, I used to be an introvert with few friends and no meaningful connections. Those days, I would not go out and befriend children in the neighborhood. Naturally, I was not much into any kind of sports. In my village where everyone was gung-ho about football, I was an anomaly. I would rather be home than being out playing football or hanging out with friends. If I was sent to any grocery store for buying supplies, I would make a straight way to the shop and immediately after the shopping, I would make a bee-line back. The same would happen if I go to the mosque as well. Not only was I frightened to meet people, I had a strange belief that spending time out, was a sign of mischievous children. If someone approached me, I would shrink to myself like a turtle pulling its head back into its shell.

My parents were super-careful about me, and they hoped that I would excel in my studies. In a sense my parents encouraged the behavior as they did not want me to go off-track. Later, the behavior got stuck, it continued to my twenties and I became a wall-flower. Being a wall-flower is tough, you get repeatedly taunted by the people and they make fun of your awkward behavior.

I remember, once a man asked me jokingly, "Muneer, what are you searching for, did you lose anything?" He was making fun of my walking without looking sideways and avoiding eye contact with people. I just smiled at him.

Do you know how I managed to change my behavior and overcome my social anxiety? When I was 24, I took a conscious decision to reinvent myself. For the purpose, first, I went to the street and stood there doing nothing. Imagine that, a socially awkward fully grown 24-year old man standing in the street doing nothing and trying to smile at everyone in an attempt to pick up a conversation. Some of my friends and villagers were confused by my strange behavior. They asked, "What happened? Anything wrong?" I said nothing, but gave a smile. It was embarrassing for me to stand in the street, however I stood because I wanted to overcome my weakness. I consciously picked up conversation with people I knew, and with their support, I made new friends as well. It was very difficult for me to face new people and talk to them, but somehow, I managed it. I continued the new habit for a few days and I am sure that it, more than anything else, has helped me to overcome my social anxiety.

There are two ways to deal with FEAR and it depends on how you define your fear. There are two different definitions possible for FEAR. Read on:

1. FEAR – Forget Everything And Run

2. FEAR – Face Everything And Rise

The first definition is for the cowards and I was not willing to believe that I was a coward. I went for the second definition, which was to look straight at my fear and face it like a boss. I started hanging out with new-found friends and started playing badminton with them. I came to be introduced to several new people at the badminton court and gradually became part of a community. Finally, I had a social address. Besides, I developed new relations with people in my village and gradually my world was opening up. Now, my primary passion is talking to people, meeting new ones and even helping complete strangers with their own personal troubles. From being a wall-flower who preferred keeping to himself, now I have become a speaker who talks to hundreds at a time and I teach students from 117 different countries. I faced my fear and conquered it. Do you think that I would have been able to overcome my social anxiety, if I did not have the courage to face my own fears?

> "The brave man is not he who does not feel afraid, but he who conquers that fear."
>
> - Nelson Mandela

Life is full of choices, not random chances. You are what you choose to be. If you choose to overcome your weakness, pay its price and face the fear, no one can stop you. The question is, "Are you ready to face your fear?"

> "Feel the fear, face the embarrassment, and keep moving forward to beat your fear."
>
> - Muneer Amayoor

33 DISSOCIATE YOURSELF FROM YOUR PAIN

"That's a perfect couple that would make everyone in the neighborhood go green with envy", said Catherine's friend when Catherine got married to her childhood sweetheart, John, and moved to their new home in the most peaceful neighborhood in the city. John was the manager at the city bank and Catherine was a successful real estate agent. Their new home with a beautiful view of the Canden Lake was, indeed, a dream house for many. At night, if Catherine took care of cooking, John took care of dishwashing and laundry and vice-versa. They had everything they wanted, reputation, a steady income and house that made others jealous. Above all, they loved each other.

However, things began to take an unexpected turn, barely three years into their marriage. John began to be frequently absent from the dinner table. Several nights, he came late, drunk. On Catherine's birthday, they had agreed to be home early and celebrate it with only themselves at home and going for a movie afterwards. Catherine reached home early on time and made preparation for the night. The movie was to start at 10 and it was already 9.30 now. John did not show up yet. Still hopeful, Catherine sat next to the birthday cake, and waited for him to arrive. As time passed and the clock struck 10, John was not yet to be seen. He would not pick her call. Tears welled up in her eyes and she became furious and melancholic at the same time. Still, she kept waiting for him. Finally, late into the midnight, he arrived, drunk and boozed up. By the time, Catherine had fallen asleep on the table. He could barely walk, she guided him to the bed and he collapsed into it. In an instant he was fast asleep in the bed with his shoes still on his feet. She was overcome with a sense of disgust.

The next day, early in the morning, When Catherine woke up from her sleep, she noticed his wallet lying on the floor. He was still asleep. There she saw something thrusting out of his wallet. She took it out and what she saw in it threw her back in shock and surprise. A picture of John sharing bed with another woman. Instantly, a wave of shock ran across her body, feverously shaking her from head to toe.

After an hour-long fierce shouting, emotionally charged outbursts, tears and abuses hurled at each other, John admitted that he had been in love with one of the employees at the bank for past two years and that they have shared bed several times. Catherine felt that the world around her just fell apart. All the time she was waiting for him, he had been making love to his girlfriend. She felt betrayed. She felt that her whole life was a mere lie, a beautiful lie. In a few weeks' time she divorced her husband. John had nothing to lose; soon he married his girlfriend. After this incident, Catehrine's life became a hell. She felt angry to everyone. Every now and then she got reminded of the betrayal she suffered. She spent hours crying like a baby. Every day, she would go back to this traumatic experience and relive it. She could never start afresh. Even 5 years after the divorce, she was still grieving and got addicted to anti-depressants and sleeping pills. Every now and then, she cursed him.

Now, pause and reflect. In this story, Catherine lost everything and she has never been able to start afresh. She could not start a new life as her ex did. Instead, her life went spiraling down with sleepless nights, perpetual anger, grief and depression. Is there a way out for her?

Yes, there is a way! Only one way out and that is to forgive her ex-husband. It is true that she cannot completely erase her memories. It is impossible. But, as long as she cannot forgive John, her traumatic experiences will keep haunting her and by repeatedly returning to the same trauma, her mind will identify with the pain. As a result, the pain becomes her. Then she defines herself in relation to the pain. She becomes identified with a victim consciousness.

If she is to start a new life, there is only one way, kill the source of pain which is her identification with her victimhood. For that, she has to let go of John. John and her painful experience with him should no longer define her. Forgiving him and taking her life into her hand is the only way to let him go. As long as he is in the back of her mind, she would keep going to the memories and pain. It would play like a loop. When you forgive by mind, a lot of chemical and emotional changes will take place in you.

Traumatic experiences are hell. However, to live with it for ever will only worsen the situation. To say goodbye to the trauma, forgive the culprit in your mind and heal your inner child. Any part of you which carries past memories is an inner child. If your inner child is wounded, take the first step to heal it now. If you need professional help to heal your inner child, do not hesitate to seek the same.

> **"Think about any attachments that are depleting your emotional reserves. Consider letting them go."**
>
> **- Oprah Winfrey**

Are you ready to dissociate yourself from past traumas and live a life with meaning and purpose?

> **"You are not the pain within you, you are what is left when you let go the pain."**
>
> **- Muneer Amayoor**

34 WRITE AND SHINE

When I feel down, I pick up my pen and diary. If I feel that I am not doing what I am meant to do, or I am not making use of my God-given talents, or I feel blank, my pen and diary act as rejuvenators. I record my thoughts as they are, in my own language. It relieves me a lot. Sometimes, I write suggestions to myself, as if someone else is writing, like "Muneer, you're a powerful person. You shouldn't feel defeated by this new challenge at your work. It's all for good. Be brave, Muneer. Take the first step with faith."

After writing, I would read it several times. It would help me affirm the idea in my subconscious mind. At times of challenges, journaling will give you wings to fly. I keep the journals with me, and occasionally go through the pages randomly. It reminds me of the milestones I have covered, the transformations I have undergone and the sea if emotions I have waded through.

> "I can shake off everything as I write; my sorrows disappear, my courage is reborn."
>
> - Anne Frank

You need not journal your thoughts every day. However, if you can do it; it is great. Develop a habit of recording your thoughts when you feel thirsty for more energy, more motivation, better clarity and sense of purpose. When you write, the fog disappears and the sky becomes clear.

> "When you write down your thoughts, you emerge as a judge of your own thoughts and actions."
>
> - Muneer Amayoor

35 WALK THE HARD WAY

It was a normal day at work. At All India Radio, Manjeri, I was busy with my work. However, nothing was normal that afternoon for me. While at work, I received a call from my father and from his voice, I could sense that something was terribly wrong.

"Son.....There are two policemen here at home.... They came looking for you....What is going on", he sounded frightened and deeply concerned, "Let me handover the phone to them", he said.

"We're from the CBCID, we have got a complaint about you.", my heart skipped a few beats. You might wonder what is CBCID, it stands for Crime Branch-Crime Investigation Team, it is an undercover investigation team. Why is the CBCID at my home? What do they want? What crime did I do? I was full of questions.

A polite and smart officer talked to me over the phone.

"We have received a complaint about you and it is a serious complaint." I was scared out of my wits and I wondered what serious crime have I committed. "The complaint points at your possible terrorist links." My phone almost fell down from my hand and I nearly jumped out of my skin. Terrorist? Me? To be alleged of terrorist link itself was worse than the most frightening nightmare I ever had. In a second, the pictures of many innocent men jailed for wrongly alleged terrorist links flashed in my mind. Oh, God, am I going to join them? If jailed for alleged terrorist links, whether or not you are innocent, you could be imprisoned for years without even any trial. I mustered up all my courage and explained to the officer that I never had any link with such organisations or persons. Much to my relief, the police man said, "We know sir, we have done our homework and enquiry into all your contacts. We know that you are clean". Besides, the officers under cover had made enquiries about me in my village as well. They could gather only positive information about me. However, before I was given a formal clean chit, the enquiry process continued for a few days and they questioned me on various matters. With frequent police questioning and seriousness with which the officers handled the enquiry, for me, my life seemed like a page from a popular Bollywood film. I could not even believe it was happening for real. But it was, sadly. I was frightened like never before in my life. Later, sitting alone in my room, thinking about all the possible directions the enquiry could go, I thought to myself, I have done no crime. Then why should I be concerned? The thought comforted me in great deal. Yet, we have plenty of examples of people who are wrongly alleged of terrorist links and spent their days in prison without any trial. The fear was real and well-grounded. However, the fact that I am innocent gave me courage.

Now, to be frank, it was not the only incident of the sort. Somebody had sent a bunch of serious complaints about me to various departments. Complaints, enquiries, questions and clean chit. The pattern was repeated several times, each time a new department though. Let me tell you one thing, going through the nail-biting questioning sessions and enquiries were like a nightmare for me and finally your innocence being proven, it is an ordeal people have rarely to undergo. However for me, I underwent the same ordeal, several times.

I do not know who made the bogus complaints against me. However, I am sure that, that person wanted to seriously disrupt my life. This is what is life; you will have to deal with people having unpredictable motives. If you want to lead a life with no challenges, then there is only an easy way – do nothing at all. If you do something creative, something useful, something inspiring, then there is every chance that you may get thrown into troubles you never anticipated. The more challenges you find on your way, the more creative and the more of a change maker you are. Be brave, face challenges and emerge as a winner.

Whoever was behind the bogus complaints against me, I do not harbour any grudge against him. Apart from forgiving him, I am greatly indebted to him for throwing a series of challenges at me. It was a tough time, to tell the truth. Yet thanks to his complaints, I learned a lot and he has made me stronger and better at facing challenges. Thanks to him, I feel, come what may, I will stand my ground.

> **"Every adversity, every failure and every heartache carries with it the seed of an equivalent or a greater benefit."**
>
> **- Napoleon Hill**

When life tests you, never concede your defeat. Keep moving forward. If you have a purpose and a strong vision, nobody can stop you.

> **"To live an easy life without challenges, criticism and troubles, there is a super easy way – stay silent, do nothing fruitful and sleep tight."**
>
> **- Muneer Amayoor**

36 LET IT GO!

Some tribes in India use an ingenuous technique to trap monkeys. The trap is simple. A hollowed out coconut with a tiny opening or a pot with a bottle neck chained to a stump will be placed on the ground. Inside the pot or the coconut will be placed some rice or berries. Attracted by the bite, the monkey will put its hand in through the tiny hole. The hole will be big enough for the monkey's unclenched fist to go through. At the same time, it will be small enough that the clenched fist cannot fit through. Once the monkey grabs the rice or berries inside, its fist will be clenched and it cannot be pulled out without unclenching. Evolution has taught the monkeys to never let go the berries in their hand. As a result, despite their desperate attempts, the monkeys will get trapped.

The trapped monkey can free itself easily if it unclenches its fist and lets the rice go. But they never do that. As a result, they end up being someone else's dinner.

Some people are just like the stupid monkeys. They never let go, no matter what. They could save a lot of embarrassment and regret, if only they let go their pride, their ego or their sense of superiority for a while. But they will not. If only they give up their pride for a second or so, they would be able to deescalate a situation. They may stand to gain a lot just by keeping mum for a while. But, their ego will not allow them. To save yourself and to gain something, sometimes you will have to make some sacrifices. To increase your profit, you have to invest more, you have to let go some money in the first place. To spend some time with your family, you may have to lose some profit. To grab more, you need to free your hand first.

> **"Price is what you pay. Value is what you get."**
> **– Warren Buffet**

We all have our hand caught in some traps of our own and we all have to let go something, if we want to make progress. Identify that which you have to lose and get ready to drop it. Or get ready to follow the monkey's suite. Let it go!

> **"Take that chisel in your hand and cut off the unwanted from you."**
> **- Muneer Amayoor**

37 BUSY AND YET BE PRODUCTIVE

Do you think that you have no time to learn new things since you are super busy at work? You work for 6 days a week, then, where is the time to learn? If this is your concern, it is time to change the perspective. Look at it this way. If you had seven days at your disposal to learn a particular portion, you would get lazy, thinking that you have more than enough time. When there is only one day, you would automatically be aware of it, and your subconscious mind will drive you to learn faster. In my case, I feel that I am more productive on my busy days. Otherwise, I just spend time at home watching videos on my mobile phone. If I am busy and I have a lot of work to do, then I shift myself into the top gear. Everything runs smoother. I can easily switch from one task to another with great ease. Above all, limited time frame would help me focus all my concentration on the work at hand. I would say, by being busily engaged with something positive, we can be more productive.

> **"Each step you take reveals a new horizon. You have taken the first step today. Now I challenge you to take another."**
>
> **– Dan Poynter**

To have luxury of time means you have your doors open for distractions. If you feel that you are running out of time, you would be able to channelize all your time, energy, concentration and brain-power to complete the task on time. So, now onwards, no more complaining about being busy. The more busy you are, the more productive you would become. Most importantly, it is not enough to get busy. The question is, are you busy with the right things? If you are busy at wasting time, sorry, no use at all!

> **"The busier you are with constructive endeavours, the more productive you become."**
>
> **- Muneer Amayoor**

38 NEVER LOSE SIGHT OF REALITY

"No more.... I'm tired man, I'm tired... How many times I tried...I don't have luck on my side...I quit... You need luck as well... I don't have it...I quit."

You must have heard similar words from many. I have. Those people who, despite their hard work and best efforts, fail every time they try. More than any group of people, they have made me think more. In spite of planning, hard work and even following all success principles, they fail to achieve their goal. If you see their diary, you can see big goals written down with deadlines to accomplish them. When it comes to their real life, they would not have reached any near their goal.

Before you set your goals, first, you should have your feet set right in the ground. Respect the ground realities and take them into your consideration when you set your goals. If you set unattainable goals for you, you would probably end up grieving and it could even eat into your confidence level, eventually causing you to quit. When you lose sight of reality, confidence will be replaced by overconfidence, reality will be replaced by imagination and rather than being guided by your intellect, you will end up being guided by your imaginative faculty which disregards the ground reality. Well, this is not to suggest that creative thinking, imagination and confidence are a threat to achieving your goals. They are not. But, if your imaginative and creative faculty have no sight or reality, it could probably throw you to dark pits. If you over estimate what you can accomplish in a year, probably, you will end up accomplishing just a quarter of it. Your goals will laugh at you.

Now let us come to the practical part. What can you do to make sure that you do not fall into this category of people? Take note of the following points.

- Before setting your goal, analyse your abilities and resources and set your goals accordingly.

- Ask yourself if you have the abilities and resources needed for accomplishing your goal.

- If you fall short of any abilities or resources, look for ways to make up.

- Do not let blind imagination cloud your judgments. Respect the ground realities.

- Accept the fact that there is no universal strategy to follow. Depending on your circumstances, you have to develop your own strategies. Don't disregard the opinions of people with great deal of experience.

- If you have a role model to follow, do not fall to the trap of doing what he/she is doing today. Instead try doing, what they were doing when they were in your stage. Meantime, never forget that you need to develop your own strategies.

- Do not blindly copy anyone. You are unique, your circumstances are unique. Respect your uniqueness.

> "If you want to be happy, set a goal that commands your thoughts, liberates your energy and inspires your hopes."
>
> \- Andrew Carnegie

Think big and be realistic. Your dreams should have two wings, reality on the one side and creative imagination on the other. Recipe for success includes these three: reality, creativity and planned heart-work. When alone, none of them would make any difference. When combined they would do wonders and you will not have to blame lack of luck. Luck is what you get when you combine these three.

> "Imagination becomes reality only if it is coupled with commonsense and a sense of reality."
>
> \- Muneer Amayoor

PART TWO

LOOK INWARD

39 OBSERVE YOUR THOUGHTS

Have you ever tried observing your own thoughts? If you try enough, you can and it is a great experience. More importantly, it will help you take charge of your mind. Like an eagle in the sky scanning the ground below, you can be an observer of your thought, a watcher of you mind and you can be the traffic police in control of the traffic of your thoughts. Now, how can you do it?

Find yourself a calm place to sit undisturbed, close your eyes, take a couple of deep breatsh and listen to the voices from distance. You should be able to hear, the birds singing, distant sound of the horn from the faraway highway, and your neighbour shouting at their kids. A cacophony of varied sound from distance. Try to isolate one of them and hear no other sound. Gradually, tune your ears to listen to the sounds less and less distant. First try listening to the sounds in your own home, your mom talking to someone else, your clock ticking, your laptop's fan spinning. Focus your complete concentration on those smaller sounds until they seem to be so loud. Then listen to your own breathing. Take long, deep breaths and feel your chest expand and shrink. Listen to its sound, listen to your heart beat. Hear nothing else. When you feel that how difficult it is to breathe, you should know that you are in a state of deep meditation. Then, think about nothing. Absolutely nothing. It will not be easy, but try. As you try this, you will find yourself looking at your mind from above. Do not let any thought come in yet. Sooner or later, when any thought breaks your vigil, you will be able to see it crawling into your mind. Observe that thought of yours. Like a bird watcher, be a thought watcher. Sooner or later, you will be able to see this thought gradually give way for another thought. Do not interrupt yet. Let them come and go and watch them as they come and go. If you are able to do it, you have succeeded in being a watcher of your mind.

Once you become a watcher of your thoughts, it will be easy taking control of your thought's traffic. Once in this state, you can empty your mind any moment you want. You would become aware of your thoughts and will be able to take control of them. You can show red light to a particular thought, stop it and bring on a new positive thought.

Now, let me come to the practical benefits of being a thought watcher. Well, the first benefit is that it helps you to take control of your thoughts and mind. If you can take control of your thoughts, you can take control of your own life. After all, you do what you think and you are what you think. It will help you to control your thoughts to your benefit. For example, if you are addicted to something, be it mobile phone, porn, liquor or substance, you can use this technique to gain control over your thoughts. Be a thought-watcher and label your addictive thoughts in red. When the thought to smoke pops up in your mind, observe that thought crawling into your mind and see what it does to your mind and how it forces you to act in certain way. Watch that thought, be a witness to its manipulations and let it go just the way it came. Being a thought-watcher stops you from making any quick response to your thoughts. Instead, like a traffic police in charge of the vehicles that come and go, you can be the traffic controller of your thoughts.

> "We are what our thoughts have made us; so take care about what you think. Words are secondary. Thoughts live; they travel far."
>
> - Swami Vivekananda

Be a thought-watcher and take hold of your mind's steering wheel.

> "Install a traffic light in your brain to control your thoughts. Let the red light blink when negativity pops up. Let the green light give you the signal to move on with the right thought."
>
> - Muneer Amayoor

40 LIFE MIRRORS YOUR SOUL

A young man asked to a Guru, "I want to shine in everything, in every aspect of my life. People should look at me with respect. I must be the No.1 in my business, family and in everything. Please bless me."

Guru replied, "Please wait, son. I will gift you a special device, which will keep you at the top all the time." He went inside home and returned with an old wooden box. The eyes of the young man shined out of hope and surprise. Guru handed him the box. When he opened it, he found nothing in it, but a mirror which reflected his own face. He looked at the Guru with a questioning countenance.

Guru smiled and said, "Son, it is your thoughts, mindset, attitude, character, humility, beliefs and spirituality that help you to shine outward. You're nothing, but an outer reflection of your inner world."

> "Attack the evil that is within yourself, rather than attacking the evil that is in others."
>
> – Confucius

Now, pause, and ask yourself, if you had a mirror which will reflect your inner self, how would it look like?

> "Look inside to shine outside."
>
> \- Muneer Amayoor

41 THE WAKE-UP CALL

Yesterday, you went to sleep in the comfort of your home. This morning, you woke up from the sleep. You opened your eyes and walked yourself to the bathroom. You brushed your teeth and had your fill for the breakfast. Now, you are reading this book. If you do not know how incredibly blessed you are, take a good look at the following statistics.

- According to the statistics, each day, 150,000 people die worldwide. You are one of the luckiest people to be alive at this moment.

- According to the World Hunger Index, 820 million people are undernourished. You are one of the luckiest people to have you fill for today's breakfast.

- Statistics say that 150 million people around the world are homeless. You are one of the luckiest few people to have a shelter to sleep tonight.

These are official figures, the actual figures may double or even triple. If you are able to read these words, take note, around the word, a total of 287 million people are illiterate. You are one of the fortunate people to be able to go to the school and learn to read and write. If you are reading this book on your Kindle, Smartphone or laptop, be thankful that you are not one of the 940 million people around the globe who do not even have access to electricity. Imagine a day without electricity, how terrible would it be for you. To know how incredibly lucky you are, take a good look at this figure. The scientists estimate that the probability of your taking birth is around just one in four hundred trillion. Now read the previous sentence one more time. This time take your time.

Having lost ourselves in this world of never ending desires, we fail to appreciate how incredibly lucky we are and as a result, people feel depressed and some even take their life. Come on people, take your life? Seriously? How blind you have to be to think that you are a loser? If you are comfortable enough to find time to read this book, you are rich, you are fortunate, you are lucky. YOU ARE BLESSED. Get it.

> "A rich man with poor mindset will end up being poor, and a poor man with rich mindset will never remain poor."
>
> – Farookh Sensei

Now, let me ask you one thing. How blessed are you?

> "Happiness is a state of mind and so is sadness."
>
> - Muneer Amayoor

42 ALL THAT GLITTERS...

Imagine you mix sugar with sand and drop them here and there on the floor. What would happen afterwards is anyone's guess. A battalion of quick response team from the nearby ant colony would rush to the scene. But will the ants carry both the sugar and sand grains to their colony? No. It is true that sand-grains and sugar-grains look alike, but the ants never get confused. They know what they need, they know how to identify what they need and they never end up carrying a single grain of useless sand to their colony. They would even identify the sugar-grains hidden underneath the sand and take it home. The ants' quick response team would work so effectively because they know what they are looking for and they know how to identify the same. They look for sugar, and they get it. They know that all that glitters is not sugar.

In today's world of credit cards and online shopping where buying any product is just a click away, I think we have a lot to learn from the ants. With so many online stores and so many products to choose from, some people end up buying everything they see, and subscribe to every service that they come across. Without a second thought, they would order expensive gadgets that they would not even care about after one or two weeks. By the end of the month, their salary would run out and they would start digging into their little savings or end up incurring debt. Is there a way out? Yes, there is.

Like ants identifying sugar from the mixture, you should be able to find out the products/services that you truly need. Like the ants, know what you need and know how to identify them. Do not fall for the advertisements. Advertisements are specially designed to make special psychological impact on you. Advertisements on the TV and social media tap into your brain's innate quality of being immediately affected by the visual images. Due to the immediate brain response to the visual images, you will soon be overwhelmed by a manufactured need to buy the product being advertised. There will be unbelievable discount offers as well. Understand that just because something is up for grabs at a low price, it does not mean that you need it. It only means that the seller needs you to buy it. Before you press that "buy now" button, think twice, ask yourself, whether you really need it.

People often commit blunders when they subscribe to online products and services like premium videos, audiobooks, gaming, music, books etc. Before hitting the subscribe button, think thoroughly. Firstly, before hitting that subscription button, ask yourself, "Do I really need it? If yes, how long?" Would you buy an excavator simply because you need to move some rocks from your backyard? No. You would simply hire one as you do not have a regular need for it. Apply the same logic to online subscriptions as well. Subscribe to a service if and only if the service is required to you on a regular basis. That is, you should not subscribe to a background music service, just for adding it to three or four YouTube videos that you publish a year. For that, you have the option either to use free stock music or you can even purchase music tracks, which will definitely cost you less than the subscription amount.

Secondly, when you subscribe to an online service, it is not only the cost and your need that you should consider. Give a serious thought about how subscribing to a particular service could affect you. To illustrate an example, if there is a subscription plan for a gaming website, there would be both monthly and yearly subscription options. If the monthly charge is 10 USD, the yearly charge would be only around 60 USD. Seeing this unbelievable fifty percent discount for a yearly subscription, your jaw may drop, and you might hit the subscription button without any further thought. You will forget to consider the question, "How a 12-month long subscription to a gaming website could affect me?" Probably, you would get addicted to the game and everything else in your life would have only the second priority afterwards. In addition to the mental cost of the addiction, your daily life would be permanently affected. The cost of the damage done to your family and life would far exceed the fifty percent discount you availed.

> "Don't tell me where your priorities are. Show me where you spend your money and I'll tell you what they are."
>
> - James W. Frick

All that glitters is not gold. Learn to find your gold. Be like the ants that never mistake sand-grain for sugar.

> "Pre-shopping thought could save a lot of post-shopping regrets."
> - Muneer Amayoor

43 THE UNINVITED GUEST

"Oh my God... How beautiful! It's an impeccable choice, dear Priya. You've bought such a beautiful bracelet for my child", said Babitha to her long-time friend Priya. "I know your taste, Babi.. I knew what you would love for your kid...ha...ha", Priya replied

Eager, to talk to all her friends at once, Babitha went talking like a radio turned on. "By the way, Neenu, what's your little sister up to these days? Did she complete her course?" Often, she could not wait for others to finish, she kept shooting silly queries at her friends. "I see that shy smile on your face Rahna, you must be living your dream with your husband. It's a shame I couldn't be there for your function".

After a long five months' gap, Babitha was finally able to meet all her close friends, who paid her a surprise visit. She was the head of the gossipers' club in the campus, and with her pregnancy, she hasn't been to the college for the past five months. She had a lot to catch up with!

With her excitement, she had almost forgotten about her 2 months old daughter, Liya who was in one of her friends' lap.

"What did you name her?", asked Sherin.

"Oh, we call her Liya. It was her father's...... father's ch.... ch... cho"

Babitha could barely finish her sentence. Suddenly, she felt that something was pulling her tongue in. In a matter of a second, her face turned pale, sweat appeared all over her body, eyeballs rolled up, she felt dizzy, She passed out and fell on the floor. Her friends rushed to her help and Priya placed her head on her lap.Yet, before they could do anything, Babitha's breathing had ceased, her heart beat had come to a sudden halt and the helpless friends had to watch their beloved friend breathe her last. Later, it was known that Babitha had a silent heart attack that took her life.

Death has a way of catching us off guard, surprising us with its cold touch and freezing us to death. Babitha, for sure, was not ready for her death. Her three-month old baby still needed her, and she left this world with an unfinished sentence.

Imagine yourself in Babitha's stead. If death comes in, as an uninvited guest, are you prepared to face it? What plan do you have to sustain your family if you have an unexpected appointment with death? How would the news be received by your dear ones? What will you be remembered for? What footprints would you have left in this world? Will your children have to take care of the debt you incurred? Will you leave this world with any unfinished sentence as Babitha did?

Remember, rarely does the death announce its arrival. And it could come, the next moment, the next minute, the next hour, the next day, the next month or the next year. It will come for sure. Who knows if I could finish this chapter you are reading now. Who knows if you could finish reading this sentence you are reading now?

"Death closes all"

–Alfred Lord Tennyson

Are you ready for your appointment with death? It could be any moment!

"Your footprints tell your story to the world."
- Muneer Amayoor

44 STRESS IS NOT ALL BAD

Stress. Is stress bad for you? Will it diminish your productivity? Is stress your enemy? The answer is a big No-No.

Imagine a cheerful and carefree student. What would happen if he/she is not the least worried about the upcoming exam? Will a happy-go-lucky guy care to prepare for his exam? No! Now, what about a carefree-going Olympic athlete? If an Olympic athlete does not show and feel any speck of anxiety, will he be motivated to bring out his/her best performance? Again, the answer is, NO.

Too often, the word "stress" is erroneously equated with "distress" and "depression". Much of the negative thoughts associated with the word, comes from this misappropriation. Scientifically speaking, there are two kinds of stress-distress and eustress. Distress is bad for you as it might leave a person unable to adapt to the surroundings which could result in mental and physical sickness. Distress might even speed up the ageing process. On the other hand, the word eustress itself means, "beneficial stress". How can stress be beneficial to someone? Don't give me that look, let me explain.

Physiologically, stress means increased production of a few hormones, namely Adrenaline, Nor-adrenaline and Cortisol. Well, you might wonder, if the increased production of these hormones is bad for you. No. In fact, these hormones are good for you and could even make you more effective. Stress could make you more effective? Yes. It can, to understand better, read on.

Imagine our days back in the woods, long before the invention of agriculture, when we were hunters and foragers. Imagine one of those distant relatives of ours going on a hunting expedition with his unsophisticated, primitive weapons. At that time when we were not on the top of the food chain, the hunter could become the hunted any moment. Imagine, while chasing a prey, he happened to bump into a voracious lion. The hunter has only two options before him-to fight or to run for his life. Either fight the lion with his primitive tools – stones, spikes, tooth and nail. Or, run away as fast as possible. Whatever he chooses to do, he needs more energy, more breath, increased concentration and a heart beating faster. Well, will that happen without any trigger? No. The hormones we mentioned earlier- Adrenaline, Nor-adrenaline and Cortisol take charge of this function. This means that, if the ancient hunter was to stand any chance, he should have experienced a momentary stress which would empower him to fight or run away from the hungry lion. Here, experiencing stress would rescue him from the jaws of death. In that sense, stress not only makes you more energetic and effective, it can even ensure your survival. This is not to suggest that stress is all good. It is not. A persistent stress, in other words, if these hormones stay high in your blood for a long time, it could pose serious threat to your mental and physical health.

It does not matter if you feel stressed for a day or two, or even if it prolongs as long as a week or so. But once the stress begins to derail your routine or take a toll on your happiness and performance, it is time to take action. When you realise that little stress is good for you, half the problem is already solved. Put stress in an alternative perspective. If you were not stressed at some defining moments in your life, do you think that you would have been able to accomplish certain feat you are proud of? If the president-elect was not anxious about the final outcome of the election, would he have worked hard enough on the campaign trail? No. I don't want you to think that I am romanticising stress and anxiety, please don't get me wrong. It must be accepted that, stress is hard to handle, let us not end up romanticising it. Call a spade a spade.

In the meantime, the benefits of the momentary stress and anxiety must be appreciated.

> "Within you, there is a stillness and a sanctuary to which you can retreat at any time and be yourself."
>
> - Hermann Hesse

If you feel that your stress level turns to distress, never feel ashamed to admit it. Seek help from your besties or experts. Tell yourself that stress is that scary dark woods which you must cross before you can reach the promised land.

> "Hello stress! Thank you for helping me to grow and shine."
>
> - Muneer Amayoor

45 BE RESOURCEFUL

Ever since the smart phones made their advent, they have become our constant companions. In its intimacy with us, it has even beaten our own shadows that follow us only when there is light or when it is day-time. What about our smart phones? Day or night, light or dark, weekday or weekend, you have your smart phones as your companion. Curiously enough, some even prefer taking it to the toilet. We use it for every sort of purpose, it has replaced our watches, our alarm systems, our flash lights, our cameras, our books, and the list goes long. Its uses are many.

Now, can you pose to reflect, what are the possible uses of your mobile phone? Please make a mental list before you read on.

To make phone calls, to browse, to play games, to check our GPS location, to navigate, to take pictures, to shoot videos, to edit photos and videos, to take notes, to record voice, to send and receive mails, to listen to radio, to read news paper, to teach and learn online, to watch news. Oh God, it is an exhausting list. However, all these are the common uses that normally pop up in your mind. Now take a different look at the question. What are the possible alternative uses of your mobile phone? What are the other alternative and creative uses of your mobile phone? Take your time to think about it. Before reading further, close your eyes, take a few deep breaths and try to imagine every alternative use you can use your mobile phone for.

I am sure that you must have come up with several ideas now. Let us take a look at a few of them.

1) Can't you use your mobile phone as a stone to throw at a stray dog chasing you? Why not?

2) Can't you use your mobile phone as a ruler to draw straight lines? Why not?

3) Can't you use your cell phone to draw a perfect rectangle? Why not?

4) If there is a tiny hole on your wall, why can't you use your phone to hide the hole so that no one can peep through? Why not?

5) Can't you use its screen as a mirror to do your hair? Why not?

6) Can't you use it as a tiny table tennis racket? Why not?

7) Can't you use it to kill a mosquito when it bites you? Why not?

8) Can't you use it as a bail on cricket wicket? Why not?

9) If you need to give your projector a little lift, why can't you place your mobile phone underneath it? Why not?

10) Why can't you use your mobile phone to crush open a peanut shell? Why not?

> "You can't use up creativity. The more you use the more you have."
>
> - Maya Angelou

When you shift the gear of your thought, immense possibilities open up before you. Now, let your imagination run riot and find more uses for your phone.

> "Resourcefulness is when your creativity serves your purpose."
>
> - Muneer Amayoor

46 OF WORK

How do the metallic gadgets rust? Why do the iron-bars turn rusty? Iron-bars and equipments rust when they are abandoned and left idle. In other words, iron rusts when it rests too much. The logic applies not only to a few metals, it could apply to you too. Like a sword that loses its sharpness when left idle, you could lose your sharpness too. Jessie, a 25 year old enthusiastic woman was diagnosed with cancer. She was one of the most active staffers in her office, she used to be the cheer-bringer at parties. But, things changed after her diagnosis, she lost hope in her life, she turned miserably dull and she was as good as dead already. Her friends and relatives thought that she would make a come-back after the treatments. To their dismay, it did not happen. Even after a successful treatment and her eventual recovery, Jessie looked the same-dull, miserable, gloomy, idle and unburnished. She did not even resume her work in the firm where she had worked before. She felt that she could not even carry herself. Every little chore seemed like a Himalayan task she could not carry out. Her clothes were seen unwashed, pile of dishes could be seen unwashed, and her house looked like a completely messed up garage. Over the time, negative thoughts had piled up in her mind and she began to slowly and gradually perish.

Her best friend, Alicia could no longer allow her friend destroy her own life. "Look at me my friend, look into my eyes and listen to what I say. I am your friend, your best friend, I have known you since we were little kids, I wish you no harm. Listen, life.... life isn't a bed of roses and you know that. Life is hard, it's hard as hell and you know that too. It will beat you down and every time you try to get up, it will try to beat you down again! That's what life is. Most times. But what keeps us going? It's only the hope and our work. Hope. Only the hope that, things could change next minute or next day or next week. This is what keeps us going. No matter what happens, if you get up and do what you should do, there is always hope. Only if you get up, only if you stand up, only if you do your work. Only if you take courage to take control of your life. You are the captain of your ship and it is you, the captain, who should decide where the ship should head. To a certain shipwreck? Or to the safety of a port? Get up Jessie! Get up and do what you should do. Better days are coming. Do you hear me? Better days are coming for you! Get up!"

After spending a couple of hours with Jessie, her friend could gradually convince her that she should get engaged in something and should not stay idle. As a starter, with her friend's help, Jessie did her laundry and dishes. Once she finished the chores, it boosted her morale and the very next day she started going to the work again where her colleagues welcomed her back to life. Slowly, she became so engaged with her works and she had no time to entertain any worries. Moreover, she started tendering to her garden, doing the much needed trimming and pruning, erecting a new fence and planting some new flowery plants in the middle. Next spring, her garden was the splashiest one in the neighborhood.

> "Your profession is not what brings home your weekly paycheck, your profession is what you're put here on earth to do, with such passion and such intensity that it becomes spiritual in calling."
>
> \- Vincent Van Gogh

How many times have you day-dreamed about winning a million dollar lottery and sitting back in your comfy chair for the rest of your life? Well, you would start dying the day you win that lottery. Being idle would kill you from within, beginning with your mind, like cancer, it would metastasize to the other parts of your body. You would lose your sharpness, your vitality, your liveliness. In no time, you would be as good as dead.

"Work is the fuel for your mind."
- Muneer Amayoor

47 STOP TRYING NOW!

Depressed. Insomniac. Miserable. Anxious. Vengeful. Haunted. Tired. These are the words that best describe Sheela's condition now. But, she had known better days. As the only daughter of a wealthy father, she was pampered by her parents and her elder brother. She had everything she ever wanted and her marriage to Sushanth was nothing less than a grand, three-day long party.

Barely three months into her marriage, her life turned into a nightmare. Though a reputed and ambitious entrepreneur, Sushanth had another face. Perhaps, a face only Sheela came to know about. "Did you think, I married you because I loved you? Hmmm, I married you because I loved your father's wealth", said Sushanth one night after beating her up. Sushanth had vicious plans and in no time Sheela's life, abused and tortured, turned into a horror film. It was a short-lived marriage, yet it gave her plenty of unpleasant and horrifying memories that still continue to haunt her. It has been five years since the divorce and yet, she spends most of her nights, sleeplessly staring at the wall, and barely eating anything. When awake, the nightmarish memories haunt her. The moment she closes her eyes nightmares haunt her. Even though she had a high paying job and luxuries, she could not enjoy her life at all. She was heart-broken.

Apart from the depression and mood-swings, she also suffered from a number of physical ailments. She has pain all over her body, frequent nausea, headache, indigestion and feverish cold. Sheela sought help from many doctors. Doctors examined her and said she was perfectly OK. Then, she tried counseling, psycho-therapy, hypnotism and a lot of other treatments. Nothing worked. What would be the reason that nothing worked for her? Why every treatment failed to cure her? Any guess?

Now, did you notice the word "trying"? She was TRYING different treatments and therapies. Note the word, "try". The word "try" only means an attempt at doing something; it does not mean the actual act of doing something. The word implies that it could, possibly, fail. You can keep on trying something without actually doing it. The two attitudes represented by the two words here, could mean a difference between success and failure. Instead of trying various treatments, Sheela has to actually take or do treatments.

"It's not that I'm so smart, it's just that I stay with problems longer."

– Albert Einstein

If you try something without believing in it, you stand to gain nothing.

Either believe, or leave.

Do, or do not!

"Stop TRYING, and start DOING."

- Muneer Amayoor

48 OF REST

When I and my team were undergoing a training programme in New Delhi, we were offered a field trip by the organisers. We were in Delhi, and we were free to choose one destination to visit, and all of us had the same destination in our mind, Taj Mahal. All of us hopped into the bus cheerfully and all danced to a popular Bollywood song all the way. A few minutes before reaching our destination, the party-mood came to an abrupt halt as our bus rammed against an auto-rikshaw. None was hurt and it was a minor accident. After dropping us at the destination, police took the bus into custody and we had to return to New Delhi by another bus.

After a couple of days, however, we came to know about an unfortunate piece of news. The bus driver who had taken us to Taj Mahal had died in another accident. Instantly, memories flashed across my mind. On our way to Taj Mahal, I and a couple of guys had befriended the driver and had small-talk with him. He was an easy-going cheerful man who liked conversing with us. In great detail, he had shared his exploits on the road. The small talk had often turned into more serious discussions as well. “I just returned from another long trip”, he had said, “After an hour’s brief nap, here I’m again, behind the wheel again!” Though he had said it with a slight tone of boasting, a sign of fatigue was visible in his eyes.

I do not know the actual details of the accident that took his life. I do not know whose fault it might have been. However, every time I am reminded of him and our Taj Mahal visit, the fact that he was seriously deprived of sleep, keeps haunting me. Sometimes, his words echo in my ears, “I don’t actually care about it. As a matter of fact, I am used to such long sleepless driving”. Sometimes, I genuinely feel that if only he had been allowed to take enough rest and sleep, his death might have been averted. It may be just a wishful thought, but the fact that he was deprived of sleep cannot be swept under the carpet.

> **“There is virtue in work and there is virtue in rest. Use both and overlook neither.”**
>
> **- Alan Cohen**

Rest is not a luxury you can live without, rest is a necessity you cannot live without. Resting-time is not rusting-time, it is essential to fuel and rejuvenate our mind, body and spirit. If you are an entrepreneur, make sure that both you and your employees get proper rest. Disregarding your employees' health for the sake of catching up with deadlines can be counter-productive in the long run. At the end of the day, it is the life that matters the most.

> "Rest is not a luxury you can live without, rest is a necessity you cannot live without."
> - Muneer Amayoor

49 THE TRIPLE FILTERS

"Since you are new here, let me tell you about our manager, first..... Something you must know to survive here.... As a person, he is good. But, as a manager, he is really a bossy type...you know that type, he just throws his weight around...and none likes him..."

On the first day at your new workplace, you must have heard such comments about people. It can be about your superiors, fellow workers or subordinates. Unfortunately, it happens most times when you become part of a new team. How should you take such comments? Should you take them seriously? Well, such comments should go in one ear and out the other. That's all.

Well, accept this fact; people are prejudiced against each other. There can be a million reasons for a person to speak ill of his boss. Samson may not like his superior James for some reasons. It can be because Samson's superior may not be Samson's type. It may be because they have a questionable history. Samson's superior may be strict about punctuality and Samson may not like that much. There can be a million reasons for Samson to speak ill of his boss. Anitha may be jealous about her co-worker's talents. Richard's co-worker may be his arch-enemy from the college days. As I said earlier, such comments should go in one ear and out the other.

Someone else's prejudices need not affect your opinions. The only way to learn about a person is to directly engage with him/her. Do not judge anyone in the first sight. Approach people with an open mind; do not let others' prejudices cloud your judgment.

Once, a man asked a monk, "I've a loose tongue. I have said a million bad things about other people. I'm not proud about it. My friends, relatives, neighbours, co-workers… my tongue spared none. What can I do? I want to repent."

The monk handed him a piece of cotton wool and said, "Please take it home. Once you reach there, pinch it off into hundred pieces and scatter them everywhere. Then come back to me next week"

After a week, the man returned. The monk said, "Go back and bring back those tiny pieces of cotton wool you had scattered. Don't forget to bring all hundred of them."

Late in the evening, the man returned with three tiny pieces of cotton."I looked for them in every nook and corner. Pardon me, I could find only three of them. The wind, water and animals took them away.", he told.

With a smile of his face, the monk said. "This is what happens with the words you pronounce. Be it good or bad, they get scattered. Especially the bad ones, they have a way of getting scattered at a faster pace. Once pronounced, you can't take them back, you can't call them back."The monk continued,"You should do a triple filter test before you tell anything about anyone."

"Triple filter? Please tell me everything about it, master", the man was curious.

"Before you blurt out anything, ask yourself three questions. Question one: Is this piece of information true and reliable? Question two: Is it beneficial for you or the other party? Question three: Is it a good thing? If you get three "yeses", proceed. Otherwise, hold your tongue.", the monk said.

Do you have the habit of bad-mouthing people? Next time you hear someone speak ill of someone else, what will be your response?

"Wise men speak because they have something to say; Fools because they have to say something."

- Plato

Have you installed the triple filter for your tongue? Seems, it is a necessary tongue-accessory for many.

> **"Holding tongue is an art very few are good at."**
> **- Muneer Amayoor**

50 BE A MYTH-BUSTER

Can you imagine an Engineering College nestled on the top of a scenic hill hundreds of meters above the sea level and surrounded by mountainous forests that are officially considered as bio-diversity hotspots? Well, the College of Engineering, Munnar where I completed my graduation is, exactly, the same. Surrounded by instagrammable landscapes and roads snaking through the mountain gaps, the area is one of the most popular tourist hotspots and a paradise for bike riders. Of all the places in the surrounding area, I was particularly curious about a place popularly known among the locals as "Chathan's Turn". Far from being a destination people would go, it is a place where people try to avoid. In fact, it is only a turn on the way from the town to the college hostel. The turn is notorious for innumerable accidents that happened here. Countless number of bikers had skidded there at night. Many of them were seriously injured. Even some of my classmates had similar experiences. It was indeed a curious turn for me. In an attempt to understand the phenomenon, I would often talk to people about the turn. But many, including some of the students would dare not talk about it.

The locally popular myth is that, the turn is cursed by a *Chathan* (a locally worshiped idol) and it is because of the curse, that bikers keep falling there. It is true that a scary idol of Chathan is installed and worshipped next to the turn, and it is also true that many people have met with accident at the so called "Chathan's Turn". So, in a sense, the belief is justified by the statistical evidence!

One night, after a party, I had to walk my way back to the hostel. On the way lies the notorious turn. My friends pleaded me not to take that way, as they believed it would put me in danger. "Muneer please don't go that way at this untimely hour. You better sleep over here tonight", said my one of my friends. Though I laughed at their advice, as I started my walk, I could sense a pinch of fear somewhere in the depths of my heart. To add to my fear, a bunch of stray dogs started to bark loudly and walk behind me. When I finally managed to reach *Chathan'sTurn*, however, I tried to reassure myself that it is only a myth and gathering all my courage, first, I walked past the Chathan's idol, and then walked past the scary turn before finally reaching my hostel.

Emboldened by my night experience, I decided to investigate into the matter. The very next day, I set out to take a close look at the place. To make it a bit more dramatic, I wore my hat, which, I believed, could make me look more like Sherlock Holmes. It is a shame that I did not have Elise Rainier's (character from the horror film franchise, *Insidious*), equipment to spot para-normal activity! Equipped or not I went there, took a close look at the place and scribbled the following observations in my pocket book.

1) Chathan's Turn is a really a vicious turn that without maximum care, any experienced rider could fall here.

2) The road here is heavily damaged and slippery gravels are all over the road.

3) There is no street light.

4) Most of the accidents took place at night.

5) Most of the victims were not natives, but outsiders who had no idea about how damaged and vicious the turn was.

Taking all these observations into account, anyone could easily conclude that the accidents have nothing to do with the Chathan's curse. With proper and timely road repair works, by erecting a street light and taking more care while driving all these accidents could be averted. The "curse" would suddenly be lifted!

I was impressed by my investigative abilities and I felt like patting on my own shoulders. Like an investigator reporting to his superiors, I presented my theory before my classmates. Some believed, and a few others told me to keep away from Chathan. Else I will be cursed by Chathan, they warned.

> "Reality is that which, when you stop believing in it, doesn't go away."
>
> \- Philip K. Dick

When you have a belief, you interpret all events to justify the belief. If you begin your investigation and observations with a theory already at hand, you would end up finding evidences to support your pre-existing theory. Instead, you should start with your evidences and then arrive at a conclusion.

> "Commonsense used in the right way will unfold mysteries."
>
> \- Muneer Amayoor

51 CAPABILITY MATTERS

A man was gasping for breath, hanging on a rope by a noose tied around his neck. He was just seconds away from the call of death. Anamika, a fifteen year old girl rushed to the scene. She asked her friend to hold the man up, and at that time, she loosened the rope around the neck. Even adults would be confused what to do when someone tries to commit suicide in front of them. What made Anamika alert?

Anamika is a Student Police Cadet from Kerala, India. She used to get trainings to tackle emergency situations. She was able to put the lessons learned into the right action at the right time.

> "God does not begin by asking us about our ability, but only about our availability, and if we then prove our dependability, he will increase our capability."
>
> \- Neal A. Maxwell

Are you confident about your abilities? Can you take the right action at the right time?

> "Capability is the capacity to use your abilities at the right time."
>
> \- Muneer Amayoor

52 OF CONTENTMENT

My first visit to the South Indian city of Chennai was instrumental in teaching me a valuable lesson. After a 24-hour long train ride from my hometown, I arrived in the city where the baking heat of sun took a heavy toll on my body. I was not used to such heat waves. Heat, coupled with high humidity made a short walk from the railway station to the nearby bus station, seem like a long mile's walk. Fearing dehydration, I bought some oranges from a street vendor and headed for my bus. When I was about to get on the bus, a young boy, may be 7 or 8 years, appeared, suddenly out of nowhere. Looking at by oranges, he extended his hand. His cracked, dry lips showed how thirsty he was. Without thinking much, I handed him an orange. Instantly, a smile appeared on his face, eyes sparkled in joy. Seeing this, a number of similar little boys and girls came running towards me. I could not help handing them an orange each. Like the first boy, they all disappeared in the crowd.

In my life, I have seen hundreds of little homeless kids sleeping on the sidewalks of busy streets.

Sometimes, I have seen those innocent little kids in the cold of winter or rain, huddled against each other for warmth, trying to sleep through the night. Winter or summer, cold or warm, rain or sun, they live out their life, with little for their sustenance. Yet, when they sleep hugging each other, they feel loved, safe, warm and secure in each others' arms, and I have seen them laugh full-heartedly and often dance in the rain. Despite their miseries, they seem to be content in their life.There is abundance in their life. Sometimes, an orange is enough to brighten their face. Sometimes, a pack of biscuits or even an empathetic look make their eyes shine

Now, what about us? Working in our air-conditioned offices, dining with our kids every day while cracking jokes, going to the bed knowing what you are going to eat for the next breakfast, playing with your kids in the lawn in our front yard, riding our dream car with our friends and enjoying all other amenities of modern life, how content are we? No, we are never truly content in our life. Our list of complaints makes a list that go too long to read through. Despite having everything at our disposal we keep on complaining. Because abundance is a feeling, it is state of mind. Not a material reality. This is not to suggest that contentment has nothing to do with money. Money is, indeed, important. But, primarily, it is state of mind.

"When you are grateful, fear disappears and abundance appears."

- Anthony Robbins

Now, stop! Stop thinking. Close your eyes. Take three long breaths and ask yourself, how content you really are in your life. What are the first five things you can do to make yourself more content?

"Contentment is not having plenty of resources, it is a resourceful state of mind."

- Muneer Amayoor

53 ENJOY EVERY MOMENT

Can you guess what could be worse than a prison sentence? If you cannot, ask people like me who lived through the year 2020, and we shall tell you that being under lockdown is a hundred times worse than a prison sentence. While imprisoned, at least, you know that you are in the prison because you are guilty of some crime. As of now, it has been around eight months since my family stepped out of the house and we are, virtually, under arrest, like millions of families around the world. You might wonder what went wrong in the year 2020. Well, by the end of the year 2019, the world was hit by a devastating pandemic called Covid-19 and in order to contain the virus spread, the whole world is currently locked down with people being allowed to step out of their houses only for the necessities. As there are elderly people in my home, we are extra-cautious about being infected. You simply spend both day and night within the four walls of your home. And you do it, every day. Every day is the same and you know that you are perfectly healthy and that you are not guilty of any crime.

Yet, you are under house arrest! If it is not worse than a prison sentence, then what else could be?

It has been around eight months since we went out for an outing with family. Covid-19 confined our life to our little world of household worries. My two year old Ridu, wife Suhra and I, we all like going out shopping and dining out in the restaurants. However, going shopping or dining out are the least of our concerns right now, nor are they wise choices at the time.

One day, my wife complained about a severe stomach pain. Given the situation, we have been avoiding hospital visits for minor illnesses too; however, as her pain turned for the worse we consulted our family doctor in our village. Since it was not cured, after the medication, we booked an appointment with a specialist in our nearby town Manjeri. Both of us were a bit anxious as a persistent stomach pain can be symptomatic of some major underlying health issues. After the consultation, the doctor asked her to take an ultrasonography of her abdomen. The moment doctor made the suggestion, the worst fears crept into our mind and she was obviously anxious as she stepped into the laboratory for the procedure. So was I. After a few nail-biting moments' waiting, we got hold of the scan result and instantly we carefully rushed through the report. Her eyes sparkled, so did mine, and we heaved a sigh of relief. Everything was normal. Nothing much to be worried. Relieved, we walked towards the doctor's cabin to show him the result. But we were asked to wait as the doctor had gone to the Operation Theatre and that he will not be available for another thirty minutes.

On the way to the waiting hall, a bright idea popped up in my mind. I turned to my wife and said:

"Wait, do you fancy dining out today?"

"You mean now?" my puzzled wife asked.

"Indeed. Right now. Come along, it's been some time", I said, pointing at the hospital canteen.

Why can't we celebrate every little moment we have? We went to the hospital canteen, ordered tea, beef fry, egg curry, vellappam and porotta.

"Forget about the pandemic for a while, see, it's a hospital, the doctors eat from here. It must be safe here", said I, as we waited for the order to be served.

"...and the scan result is fine, a celebration is in order...I guess", added my wife.

Even though it was merely a hospital canteen, we dined as if we were out in some beach restaurant. The food tasted great, for a while, the crazy 2020 seemed normal. Back in the doctor's cabin, he told that it was just a few red spots inside the stomach.

"A two weeks' medication, and you will be good", he said.

On the way back home in the car, the party-mode was on. We played our favourite songs and hummed along. As we turned a curve in the road, Suhra saw a juice shop and suggested having some. With the pandemic protocols in place, only take-aways were allowed and we took two glasses of juice to our car and with great joy sipped from them. It was a fine orange juice. The joy of having it together, sitting in the car with our favourite songs in the air, was tremendous. We converted an otherwise tiresome visit to the doctor's, to a joyous much-awaited trip.

When the Covid-19 closed the doors to dining out, roaming around, going to the park and little tours, we opened up our mind. Our mind showed ways to find joy in everything we do, like this hospital visit.

"And in the end, it's not the years in your life that count. It's the life in your years."
- Abraham Lincoln

The key to find eternal joy in our life is to start living, every moment to its fullest. Instead of waiting for the challenges to go away, you should focus on the moment you have. The only time that is real is NOW. The past is dead, the future is yet to come or you may fall dead before you complete this sentence. All you have is NOW. All you have is HERE. Living in the regrets about the past, or the paradise yet to come in the future will divorce you from the present. Instead, occupy the present, live each moment as deeply as you can. At the end of the day, only thing that is waiting for us for sure is the eternal darkness of death. Start living with what you have. NOW. Not tomorrow. Tomorrow does not exist. "Now" exists. "Here" exists.

"Sense of joy brings more life to the moment."
- Muneer Amayoor

54 ALT + CTRL + DEL

Two weeks after ordering their dream-car, Ram's family was ecstatic when they received a call from the car showroom. After what seemed like ages, the car has finally arrived in the showroom. It had taken Ram 4 long years to save enough for the car. Ram hired an auto-rickshaw and the whole family, Ram, his wife Ramya and the six-year old Ayan, went to the showroom to receive the car. The whole family posed next to the car and the sales-executive at the showroom, clicked a family portrait.

Ayan insisted he wanted to sit in the front. The three got in the car and Ram said, "Let's first go home and after the lunch let's go for a ride". "Wow, the first outing in our own car", said Ramya. The table was set and Ram and Ramya took their seat. But little Ayan was still walking around the car and looking at it from every angle. "Ayan, come in, have your lunch, we need to get going soon", Ramya called out for her son. The next moment, Ayan joined them and like a starving boy, he finished up his lunch even before his parents did.

He was super-excited for the ride and could not wait a second more. Again, he started walking around the car appreciating its grandeur from every possible angle.

After thirty minutes, when Ram was walking towards the car, he could not stand what he saw. There was little Ayan with a sharp stone in his hand going creative on the brand-new car.

"What on Earth are you doing? Scratching on the brand-new car?" Ram was burning up with rage. Blood shot up to his face and his eyes turned red. Grinding his teeth in rage, he dragged Ayan by his hand and with a stick beat him up black and blue. Ayan screamed in pain and his mother pleaded Ram to stop beating. Ram could not control his fury and went on a rampage. It was only when he got tired, he came back to his senses and stopped beating the child.

"What did you do with our child? He could not hold even a glass in his hand. Did you break his hand?", after a few minutes Ramya came running to the room and shouted at Ram. After taking a look at Ayan's hand, Ram decided to take him to the doctor's.

For the family, the much awaited first outing in their brand-new car, turned out to be a hospital visit. The X-Ray revealed that Ram had broken his son's wrist and it had to be immobilised in a cast of splint. "His wrist needs a complete rest for next 6 weeks. It's bad", said the doctor. On the way back home, none spoke a word, Ayan was weeping, tears ran down his mother's cheek and Ram tried his best to hold back his tears.

After getting out of the car, and putting Ayan in his bed, Ram went out to take a look at the car. As he approached the car, the scribbling on the car became clear. Right below the side window, it read "I lov u papa". The tears he had been trying so hard to hold back, rushed forth and he ran to his son's room, hugged, kissed and said to his little son, "Dear, I love you....I love you more than anything in the world... I am so sorry."

How good are you at controlling your emotions? When something goes wrong, go to the Task Manager, you press three keys in the Windows. Alt+Ctrl+Del. You can use the same formula to manage your emotions as well.

Alter your state.
Control your words.
Delete the negative picture.

High IQ might help you to score well in your math test, but to score well in your life's test, you need high EQ. EQ, also called Emotional Intelligence, is the ability to manage and use your emotions in a positive way in order to dissolve quick emotional responses like anger. IQ without EQ is, virtually useless. To truly succeed in your life, you need to manage your stress and emotions as well. Before you speak and before you act, pause for a second, take a deep breath and try to understand the situation and your own emotional response to it. Then make the perfect response to deescalate the situation and to benefit everyone. Remember, nothing done can be undone and nothing uttered can be taken back.

> "We are what we repeatedly do. Excellence, then, is not an act, but a habit."
>
> \- Aristotle

Be your own commander. Have authority over your state of mind, words and actions.

> "Alt+Ctrl+Del is the hotkey to end problems. Alter your state, control your words, and delete the negative pictures."
>
> \- Muneer Amayoor

55 DISSOLVE WITHIN YOURSELF

King Bheemasara of Amithpur once left the comforts of his royal palace and went to the still forests in the foothills of Himalaya. Accompanied by his royal guards, this long journey was not a regular hunting expedition, but the king wanted to meditate in the Himalayan forests. The king found an ideal place to sit and ordered his guards to station themselves away from the king so that their presence will not disturb his meditation. A couple of hours into the meditation, a lady wearing saree came running and happened to pass by. In her rush, she did not even notice the meditating king and the end of her saree happened to lightly brush up against the king's hand, awakening him from the meditation. The furious king looked around and saw the lady fast disappearing into the thick forest.

"How dare she... Ruining my meditation....?" the king murmured and ordered his guards to follow and bring her to the palace handcuffed.

"How arrogant! I will teach her a lesson.... A lesson she will never forget."

The king's men caught up with the lady and brought her to the palace the very next day. As she was dragged to the king's chamber, she could be heard screaming, "Let me go....I have done nothing... he would have arrived there by now, let me go."

"Shut your ugly mouth, lady you are in His Majesty's presence", warned the chief of the royal guard.

Collapsing on her knees, the lady repeated her chant, "Let me go, let me go". The king turned furious and said, "Look at me, the arrogant one, look straight into my eyes and tell me why did you interrupt my meditation yesterday? Couldn't you see, I was talking to the God."

"Your Majesty, pardon me, I don't know what you are talking about, I did not ruin anyone's meditation yesterday. Why would I?" the lady replied, looking up from the floor, with her hair running down her face.

"Are you arguing with your King now? Listen to me now, or I will throw you in jail. I, the King Bheemasara of Amithpur was meditating in the forest yesterday and it was you who ran past me and your saree brushed up against my hand and my meditation was ruined. I do see eyes on your face, so you did it intentionally, didn't you? Couldn't you see I was talking to the God?" the furious king erupted in rage.

"Oh, my lord, now I understand what happened yesterday. Please be kind to lend me your ears. I shall tell you what happened yesterday", the lady pleaded to the king.

"Well, now you admit your guilt. That's better. Tell me, why did you awaken me from my meditation." the king retorted.

"I am not sure what happened yesterday. Pease believe me my Majesty, I may have interrupted your meditation. I should not have done that. I must have been unaware of your presence. In fact, yesterday, I was running to meet my husband. He was away for the last ten years and he was due to arrive yesterday. The moment I knew he was on the way, I ran as fast as I can to meet him on the way. I could not just sit at home and wait for him to arrive." the lady started explaining herself. The whole court turned silent as she went on with her explanation.

"Well, it may be right, you may be telling the truth. But does that justify ruining my meditation? Tell me does that justify your crime?", king shot back.

"My Majesty, please allow me to finish. Nothing could justify my crime, I admit it. But I too was in a meditation at the time of my 'crime', and my full concentration was in it."

"What on earth are you talking about, what kind of meditation was it? I have never heard of someone meditating while running", the court burst to a sudden laughter.

The lady continued,"My Lord, ever since I heard that my husband was on his way, I was yearning to feel his palm in mine, to meet him in person after ten long years. That was my meditation. To reach him as fast as I can.That was my meditation. Nothing else bothered me, I could see nothing on my way, only his face, I was meditating on him. I am sorry my Lord, I could not see you on my way. I did not even know when I brushed my saree up against you on my way. I was running to meet him. I was meditating my Lord, I was meditating on him."The whole court fell silent and the hall reverberated with her words.

She went on,"My dear Lord, I am sorry to say this, your meditation was not as deep. Pardon me. If you were truly meditating, nothing could have distracted you. A slight touch of my saree could not have awakened you if you were truly meditating."

The king looked down in silence. All his ministers and court's men looked down in shame.

For the king, the real awakening was not when the lady's saree brushed up against his hand; it was when the lady spoke in the court. In fact, it was a rude awakening for him. Meditation is a deep state of concentration and when you are truly meditating, you would be transported to a different realm. Meditation does not mean that you have to sit straight with your eyes closed in a silent place. You can meditate anywhere. You can meditate even in a crowded train, you can meditate doing the things that you love the most, you can meditate doing the things that bring you the most joy, you can meditate listening to your favourite songs, you can meditate reading books and what not. If nothing distracts you from what you are doing, that means you are truly meditating.

> "Your vision will become clear only when you can look into your own heart. Who looks outside, dreams; who looks inside, awakes."
>
> \- Carl Jung

Now, close your eyes, take a deep breath and ask yourself how heartfelt your meditations and prayers really are.

> "The best form of meditation is when you do things that you love the most."
>
> \- Muneer Amayoor

56 COURAGE WITH SENSE

Once, when I was driving my motorbike on a busy road, a teenager boy came riding his bike from the opposite direction. There was nothing particularly noteworthy about his motorbike, just a regular bike, I noted. However, seeing the speed at which he was riding, I felt genuinely concerned for him. He was overtaking vehicles, one after another, in way reminiscent of an aggressive footballer dribbling his way through. But it was not a soccer field and I am not even sure if he reached his destination safe and sound.

You might have seen bike stunts performed by trained professionals on custom built roads. But, how will it go if amateurs imitate the same? That too, on a public road as busy as it can be! Once, two college students from Kerala tried a stunt on a public road, riding their motorbike only on a single wheel. To use the bikers' terminology, they were trying to pull off a Wheelie. It was at the same time, a car came from the opposite direction. Seeing the bike speeding up on a single wheel, the car driver was puzzled and lost control. The car skidded to a field nearby with some of the passengers sustaining injury. The bikers were equally confused as they were not expecting any traffic! The speeding bike went out of their control and they got injured too.

What is to blame here? I would say, it is the curse of learning. Learning only one percentage of something, and acting as if he/she knows everything about it! The reckless bikers would claim to be courageous, but they are not. They are troublemakers. Courage is a good quality, no doubt. However, jumping into something without thinking is a foolish act. Even in a war, the parties will not charge at the enemy without understanding the circumstances well enough, even if they are very well equipped with arms. The soldiers' first focus is on keeping the perimeter safe, not recklessly charging at the enemy line.

> **"Have courage to use your own reason!"**
> **– Immanuel Kant**

Are you able to activate your courage mode in the right way, in the right time? Or are you one of those thoughtless and impulsive fools pretending to be a daredevil?

"Be a thoughtful daredevil. Don't let the devil dare you."

- Muneer Amayoor

57 LEARNING NEVER STOPS

When Amit saw his friend Jagan riding a horse, he felt a sudden urge to ride on the horse back. "Friend, would you let me ride your horse please?" asked Amit.

"Why not", said Jagan and asked,"Do you know how to ride a horse? Do you need my help?".

"Not at all. I can do it myself.", said Amit as if he knew everything there was to know about horse riding.

Amit somehow managed to climb onto the saddle. He pulled the reins. Alas! In a split second, the horse bounced up in the air before speeding like crazy, kicking up dust and throwing Amit off balance. There lies poor Amit right on the ground, still having no clue as to what actually happened to him. It took him a while to come back to his senses.

Earlier, Amit thought that he was a master of horse riding and then, he had a rude awakening.

Now, from his experience, he understands that he has no clue about horse riding.

However, Amit took it as a challenge, and started practicing horse riding with Jagan's help. After a few months' intense practice, he mastered horse riding, making Jagan proud of his friend.

One day, Jagan was painting a picture of Amit riding a horse. He did it just to kill time. It was at that time an eminent artist happened to pass by him. The artist took a close look at the painting. "Wow!", exclaimed the artist and asked in amazement, "Did you paint this, boy?" Jagan nodded his head.

"From where did you learn painting? Who was your trainer?", he enquired.

"I haven't learned painting, I painted it just for a time-pass.", Jagan said.

"Wow", said the artist, "Well then, you have a shining spark of an artist inside you."

As for Jagan, he did not know that there was an undiscovered artist within him. After meeting the well-respected artist who spotted his artistic talent, he came to know that all along he had been blessed with a talent that he himself did not know. Jagan is an artist and now he knows it. He can now approach a master and polish his skills. What if he becomes the next Picasso? Who knows!

There are four levels of awareness. Look at the table below.

You don't know that you don't know.	You know that you don't know.
You don't know that you know.	You know that you know.

A fool thinks that he knows everything. A wise man thinks that he knows very little, and there are still a lot more to learn and master. A wise man's awareness is the key to mastery.

> "Anyone who stops learning is old, whether at twenty or eighty. Anyone who keeps learning stays young. The greatest thing in life is to keep your mind young."
>
> - Henry Ford

Do you know what are the skills you are good at, and what are the skills you are not good at?

> "The more you learn, the more you realize that you still have a lot more to learn."
>
> - Muneer Amayoor

58 TIME HEALS WOUNDS

My phone rang at 5 a.m. It was unusual. I was working at my office, All India Radio, Thrissur at that time. It was my elder brother at the other end of the phone. "Our brother's new born baby passed away." This was the news. I was shocked. Just before two days, I had received that good news about the same child's birth. I could not leave the office immediately, as I wanted someone else to take over my duty. My colleague reached there at the earliest, and I left. I ran to the town, because there were no taxies available at that time. I wanted to reach before the funeral. As I impatiently waited for the bus, every minute seemed like ages. After traveling in the bus for a while, I hoped onto the first train bounded north. Despite all the trouble I took, I could not be home before the funeral. An unusually silent home welcomed me. As I entered home, I saw my brother's wife inconsolably weeping in the bed. Everyone there found it difficult to manage their sorrow. I thought about her, she had carried her baby in her womb for nine months, then went through an excruciating pain, giving him birth and she must have weaved colourful dreams while feeding him. The baby was very healthy at the time of birth. However......God called him back after two days. We find consolation in the thought that the time allotted to him on the Earth was brief. There was nothing that the family could do, the father and mother can only hope that the time would heal the wound as it does usually.

> "Time heals griefs and quarrels, for we change and are no longer the same persons. Neither the offender nor the offended are any more themselves." - Blaise Pascal

Life is, essentially, unpredictable. Fateful incidents such as this could happen in your life too. With time, our memories gradually disintegrate and fade away. If not, our life would be impossible to bear, and we would be crushed by the weight of our memories. Time is the panacea for every wound, in time every pain would heal.

> "Forgetting is also a blessing, just like the ability to remember."
>
> - Muneer Amayoor

59 LET'S SAY SOMETHING

"Why did I do it? What was I thinking? Did I really think I can do it? How stupid I was!"

I must have cursed myself a million times for agreeing to be the student editor at the College of Engineering, Munnar. Initially, I received no support from the fellow students and I had, ahead of me, the daunting challenge of putting together a college magazine. There were times I literally cried in solitude and cursed myself for taking up the responsibility.

However, I started to make a headway once I was able to put together an efficient team. With a team of talented comrades, you could even move any mountain, right? Once the team started to function in full swing, slowly, but gradually, the magazine began to take shape and the whole process seemed a fun. Just a couple of days ago, I was cursing the day I took up the charge of magazine and now I am enjoying the same work. Besides, who wouldn't appreciate an opportunity to bunk boring lectures? Sleepless nights with little to eat, running from class to class soliciting creative works for the magazine, nights spent lying in the college lawn staring into the infinity of the sky, brainstorming for creative ideas... We enjoyed every step on the way. The goal was well defined- bring out the best magazine in the college history- and to fulfil the same, each one of us worked like a bee in a beehive. Collecting entries, editing them, type-setting, designing, soliciting sponsors, I still get goosebumps when I think about the way we worked together as a team and we were able to finish the work sooner than we expected.

As we were running low on fund, we left no stones unturned to secure the best deal for printing. The quality of the paper and the quality of the print were non-negotiable for us. We wanted the best quality printing at the lowest price possible. As the city of Sivakasi in the neighboring state of Tamil Nadu was known for its innumerable printing presses and publishers, we headed to the city and met with the owner of a press. At the press, beautifully printed books and magazines were put on display and the owner agreed to print our magazine the way we wanted it.

"See that blue magazine over there? Check it out, I shall print your magazine exactly like that", the owner said pointing at a beautifully printed magazine. We were impressed by the deal he offered. Besides, the overall cost was much cheaper than we thought. "We have a deal", shaking his hand, I said before he changes his mind. We were asked to pay the fifty percent of the cost in advance and he promised that the printed magazine will be shipped to the college address, as soon as they are printed. We agreed and returned to our college.

Even though the shipment did not arrive, taking the press owner's words to account, we announced the magazine release date and arranged lyricist Chunakkara Ramankutti as our Chief Guest. We hoped that the print would arrive on time as the press owner promised. Unfortunately, even two days before the magazine release, the shipment did not arrive and in the eleventh hour, the press authority informed us that the printing was not over yet. There was no time left to go ballistic against the press, there was no time to be upset, there was no time left to curse anyone. We rushed to a printing press at Kochi in Kerala, and got just one copy printed for the release. The moment we got hold of the print copy is still afresh in my mind. Finally, we were able to produce a copy for the release. On the eve of the release day, we set the banners, pasted posters, did the decoration works and the works got carried onto the late midnight. By the time the final works were done, we were completely exhausted. But nothing could beat the sense of accomplishment we felt. Tears of joy rushed down my cheek.

The next day, the magazine "Let's Say Something" was released. It was a grand ceremony; everyone who went through the magazine congratulated us for the good work. The magazine team was literally praised to the heaven. However, as we were still waiting for the shipment to arrive, the copies of the magazine have yet not been distributed among the students. A few days later, we received a call from Sivakasi and they informed us that the shipment will be delivered in two days' time. After two days, our team impatiently waited at Munnar town waiting for the truck to arrive. We hired an Auto-Rikshaw and rushed to the college with the stacks of magazines. Our team members were waiting there. We opened the stack and took out one magazine, turned the pages. We took the next one, then the next so on and so forth. The worst nightmare has come true. The whole team was disappointed at the very first sight of the magazine. The press owner did not fulfill his promise. The quality of the pages as well as the printing was not as he had promised. Low quality pages, low quality printing. I could not control my tears, tears welled up in our eyes. Our hard work had not been paid off, we felt cheated, betrayed and inconsolably disappointed. Though we threatened the press owner that we would file a case, he did not even acknowledge our grievances. Determined to file a case, we approached our Principal as he is the official publisher.The principal understood our grievance, sympathised with us and like us, he too wanted to file a case. However, considering how long the legal procedure could go, the Principal convinced us not to file as case as it could even jeopardise our studies.

"Hm.. see what they have done with the money... look at the paper quality. ... It's a shame",

While distributing the magazine copies, some students were muttering about the poor quality of the magazine. However, people who actually cared to read through the magazine, congratulated us for the excellent work. Those who knew our pain empathised with us and even spread the word about the betrayal.

Looking back, I would say, the most colourful days in my college life are those days. Running for articles, roaming for photographs, arranging interviews, sleepless nights spent editing, designing and above all, the deep bond that the magazine team developed among ourselves.....everything was worth it. Along the way we learned a lot, we laughed a lot, we shared a lot and we were able to prove that, together, we can move any mountain.

> **"Hope is wishing for a thing to come true. Faith is believing it will come true. Work is making it come true."**
>
> **- Dr. Norman Vincent Peale**

Sometimes in our life, you may not get the best output for your best work. However, it will give you the best memories and lessons valuable forever.

> **"The real beauty is in the process, not in the output."**
>
> **- Muneer Amayoor**

60 WAIT AND ACT

How patient are you? On a scale of ten, with one being the least patient and ten being the most patient, what would be you score?

Once, Prophet Muhamad and his disciple Ali were walking through a street. At that time, a man started abusing Ali with harsh words. Ali did not say anything back. Both of them waited patiently for the other man to stop. When Ali saw that the man had no intention to stop, he replied harshly. At that moment, prophet Muhammad walked away. Later, Ali asked prophet, "Why did you leave when he abused me? I was alone in front of my enemy." Prophet told him that when he waited patiently, ten angels were giving replies on his behalf. When Ali replied harshly, angels left. Prophet explained the reason to leave.

I have seen an office where one person shouts at his superior officer, while he listens with a smile. Even though the man behaved provocatively, the superior silently smiled without uttering a word. Later, he said to me that there was no point in talking to an angry person. An angry person can't understand logic in that state. He/she can be convinced in no way at that time. So, wise men stand away from getting into arguments with angry persons. They listen silently with a smile, and when the mood is right, they talk to him/her in a convincing way.

> **"Weakness on both sides is the motto of all quarrels."**
>
> **– Voltaire**

What is your way of dealing with angry attackers showering harsh words and showing provocative gestures? What is the first step that you have to take in order to optimise your tolerance level?

> **"Arguing with an angry person could lead to trouble, so wait and act."**
>
> **- Muneer Amayoor**

61 THE TECHNO-FASTING

"....I wanna stop it...and do you know what is the worst thing? When I wake up in the morning, even before my eyes are fully open, my hands search for my smartphone! And I would get it...That's how I start my days, every day...I wake up with my eyes glued to the smartphone.... I wanna get rid of this addiction..."

One of my friends once told me that his mobile addiction was so terrible that it affected his routine and even work. He needed help.

"You are talking to the right person. I too had the same trouble. Thank God, I got rid of it now", I replied. In fact, like many of you, I too had the same problem. Like my friend, for me too, my smartphone was the first thing in the morning and the last thing at night. In fact, several nights I have even fallen asleep with my mobile phone right on my chest or buried somewhere under my blanket. If I do not get my phone in the morning, I would feel uncomfortable.

However, now it is an old story for me. I have learned to put away my phone before sleeping, and not to grab it immediately after waking up. In my case, I started enjoying life more after losing this habit. Besides, having lost the addiction, it seemed like my days were stretched by hours and I had time for everything. More than anything else, I witnessed my productivity skyrocket. I'm sure, you too can experience it.

To solve any issue, we need to hit directly at the root-cause. The same is true about this trouble as well. Why does mobile phone usage become such an addictive habit? The answer is simple-our curiosity. Human beings are, basically, curious by nature. We are curious to know, what is going on around us, we are curious to know what is happening with other people's lives and most importantly, we are curious to know how others perceive us. Social media mainly taps into these innate curiosities of ours. Many of us log into the social media accounts to know what the latest trending news is. We are curious to know how many people have liked or responded to our latest social media post. We seek to peep into other people's private life by closely following their posts. Everyone likes to project a happy and enviable life before our friends and relatives, with social media and instant messaging services at hand, projecting a glamorous life has become easier than ever before. Understand the fact that our brain enjoys the whole process as these activities increase the dopamine level in your body. Dopamine is, simply put, one of the happiness hormones. Every addictive habit, including smoking, has the same mechanism at work-when you are engaged in your addictive behaviours, be it excessive mobile phone usage, be it smoking, be it drinking, be it watching porn or whatever, Dopamine level shots up in your body and it makes you momentarily happy. The brain, having tasted its delicacies, will keep asking for the same and that is how you get addicted to the habit.

To get rid of your mobile phone addiction, first acknowledge the fact that it is as serious as any other major addictions. The same mechanism and the same hormone are at work and as a result, you cannot get rid of the addiction, all of a sudden. It has to be done, slowly and gradually. Here in this chapter, let me propose a scientific approach that would definitely help you to get rid of your mobile phone addiction.

Now let me tell you a practical method you can follow, a method that worked for me. Once in every week, take what I call "techno-fasting". Every week, one day, say "No" to your mobile phones and gadgets. Believe me, it will not be as easy as it sounds. You are dealing with an addiction, respect that fact. But try. After three to four weeks, you would gradually get used to it. That does not mean, you are done with the addiction. It is only once in a week now, gradually, increase the frequency of your techno-fasting and soon you will notice its benefits. The fasting will help you detox tour brain by keeping Dopamine level normal and you will see that days are longer and you have plenty of time to explore yourself, to get engaged in other activities and most importantly, you will be able to enjoy the sunrise and sunset without the distraction of the mobile phone. As I said, it will take time. For me, it took time and I have been sober ever since.

The technology is meant to help you. Of course, it could help you if and only if you have control over it. If your electronic devices are controlling you, if they decide your routine and steal your time, you should know that you are not in control.

> "Never confuse motion with action."
>
> – *Ernest Hemingway*

Now, tell me my friend. When are you planning to observe your "techno-fasting"?

> "Depending on how you use it, technology can upskill you, or just kill you."
>
> - Muneer Amayoor

62 TIME AND PATIENCE

He was an old arrogant king who used to make trouble by making unrealistic orders. Everyone had to follow his orders or be prepared to die. He enjoyed being cruel. He had a grudge on one of his ministers for some reasons even unknown to him. One day, during the royal meeting, he called the minister and told him, "Hey, look at this glass pot. And look at this gold fish in it. You have to make it speak...., or get ready to die." Everyone in the meeting was shocked. After a few seconds of silence, the minister replied humbly, "I will make the fish speak, however I need one month's time to train the fish.". The king agreed with a laugh. He was sure that the minister would fail in the test and he will be finally able to cut his throat.

On the way back home, the minister's friend asked him, "Why did you assure him that you would make the fish speak, is it humanly possible? He is going to kill you". The minister smiled at him and said, "I have asked him for one month's time. Did you notice how senile and ill he has become over the past few weeks? By the one month's time, either the old king will die, or I will find an idea to win the game."

> **"The two most powerful warriors are patience and time"– Leo Tolstoy**

Time will give you the solution to all your challenges. The question is simple and direct. Are you willing to wait patiently without accepting failure at the face of the first hurdle itself?

> **"Stay calm and let the time do its magic"**
> **- Muneer Amayoor**

PART THREE

SPREAD OUTWARD

63 FAMILY FIRST

"What would you do if you knew that you had only 24 hours more to live?" Once, I asked this question to all my online students from different countries. They were from diverse backgrounds with 117 different nationalities. Yet, there was one thing common in everyone's reply. They made it crystal clear that they wanted to spend the final hours of their life, with their loved ones- family and friends. Now, what might be your answer?

Sometimes, we get caught in the madding crowd; life becomes a mere hustle, shuttling between places, rushing to meet deadlines, chasing clients for your business and above all mundane everyday conundrums. All along, you forget about the ones that matter the most - your soulmate, kids and parents. Your little kid would be yearning for a hug from you, parents for a caring touch, and soulmate for a loving kiss. But, you have other priorities, your work on thickening your wallet.

Money is needed, no doubt. However, a time-mapping is needed where you consciously assign quality time for your family. What is quality time? It is the time spent together, with occasional loud bursts of laughter, giggles and chit-chats. It is dining together around the table of love. It is playing with kids, and going on a tour trip with the soulmate and parents. It is a family dinner table where worries about your balance sheet dare not encroach. If your children have to repeatedly appeal for your attention because your eyes are glued to your screen, wondering about the implications of the business mail you just received, it is not a quality time with your children. To have quality time with your family, you need to be fully present in the present.

> **"A Happy Family Is An Earlier Heaven."**
> **- George Bernard Shaw**

It is time for introspection. What are the five immediate changes that you should make in your habits and schedule, in order to reserve abundant quality time with your family?

> **"Do you spend quality time with your family and loved ones? If not, remember, money buys, but not love."**
> **- Muneer Amayoor**

64 SMILE CONNECTS YOU

A girl was standing a jump away from a railway track. She had lost all her hope in life and it was evident that she was about to commit suicide. Two people walked by, they looked at her and asked, "What's wrong?" She did not reply. They passed by. When only 5 minutes were left for the train's arrival, a young student was passing by the girl. He smiled at her, a gentle smile, and looking into her eyes, asked, "Dear friend, what's wrong with you?" Instantly, she burst into tears sobbing like a child. The boy gave her ears and she poured her heart out. She walked back to her life with a smile on her face.

> "A simple smile. That's the start of opening your heart and being compassionate to others."
>
> – Dalai Lama

Just think, why the first two persons were not able to connect with the girl?

"Connect with a smile and communicate with your heart".

Muneer Amayoor

65 LOVE, AND SHOW YOUR LOVE

There is a disturbingly moving story titled, "Neyppayasam", written by Kamala Surayya, an Indian writer. The title, in fact, refers to a popular pudding in Kerala. The story is about a family with a husband, wife and their three children. It was after two years of romance that the two had got married against the wishes of their family. However, with three children and repeated financial troubles, their relationship had long lost its initial warmth. Drudgery of domestic chores had made her less available for small talks, persistent financial worries and office works had made him rather indifferent. They passed by each other saying no word. They had long forgotten to appreciate each other for their little achievements. Still they loved each other One day, when the husband returned from the office, he found his wife lying dead on the floor. The children were too young to understand the meaning of death. That night, worried about what the children would eat for dinner, he took them to the kitchen. Before her death, she had prepared different food items for them to eat. In one of the pots, was found "Neyppayasam" (a special hot pudding). Children began to sip from Neypayasam. “Don’t you need rice, son?”, asked the father. Son replied, “No, the Payasam is so tasty”. “That’s right, mom has cooked such a delicious Payasam for us”, said the second son. Unable to hide his tears from the kids, the father, immediately went to the bathroom.

The story poses a serious question before us the readers. The mother used to work 24x7 caring for her husband and children. She found joy in it. She used to cook their favourite dishes every day. But, the husband had long ceased passing any pleasing comments and children were not old enough to appreciate her for the good meals she used to cook. All her life, she cooked tasty dishes and never did she hear a good word from her loved ones. Now that she is dead and when her children and husband are finally able to appreciate her for her love and care, she is no more there to witness it. Her husband is finally able to shed tears for her, but what difference does it make? He and children finally appreciate her love and care, but what difference does it make? She cannot hear a thing anymore, she cannot see a thing anymore. She cannot feel their love anymore. She is dead. She is gone.

One day, my wife cooked a special vegetable dish for me to take to my office. Usually, during the lunch break our office turns into a small party hall where everyone would share their food with each other. My colleagues are a bit noisy when it comes to the party time. Anyway, the day my wife cooked the special vegetable dish, my colleagues profusely praised my wife's cooking skill. "This is from a master chef", said one of them. I was so delighted to hear that. Later, I called my wife on phone, congratulated her, and shared the happy news with her. I could sense a delightful surprise and a peculiar energy in her voice. Over the phone, I could not see her, but I could imagine an instant smile appearing on her face, a gleeful smile.

Everyone around you is yearning for a word of appreciation or love. Out of 1440 minutes a day, why can't you reserve a minute, just one minute, to show a gesture of love and appreciation for your loved ones? What do you stand to lose if you appreciate someone for a good thing they have done? You will lose nothing. But for them, it may make their day, it may energise them, it may make them feel valued, it may revitalise them and it may help them grow faster, better and sharper. At what cost? At the cost of just a word, a word of appreciation or a gesture of love.

> "*If all you did* was *just look* for *things* to *appreciate,* you would live a joyous, spectacular life." -Abraham Hicks

Now, can you take up a challenge? A simple challenge that would cost you nothing. Can you exchange at least 10 words of love and appreciation to those around you every day?

> "Show your love and appreciation while you can."
>
> \- Muneer Amayoor

66 EAT AND MEET

Did you know that you can make those boring marriage receptions you have to attend, a lot more funny by observing people's dining habits? If you didn't, try it. Believe me, it works.

Once, I attended a marriage function. Buffet dinner was supplied at the party. Different dishes ranging from soups and salads to Biriyani rice and fried chicken with a lot of other items, the names of which are unknown to me, were served! Apart from having small-talk with my dining partners, I have a curious habit of observing other people's dining style. Believe me, It is fun watching other people eat!

At the party I mentioned earlier, I saw a young man approaching the buffet table with a plate, then filling it with all the items on the table, in addition to grabbing a lot of little pots filled with sweets and desserts. It was all the courses in just one go-from appetisers to the deserts- all in one go. I thought that he must be afraid if the items would run out by the time he finishes the first course. Or, may be, he had a voracious appetite. Whatever, it looked like he was carrying a hill in his palm. Just kidding, guys! However, you also may have witnessed such scenes at many parties, haven't you?

Dining is an art. It is also a culture, which varies from place to place, culture to culture and religion to religion. For example, if it is an Iftar Party, the practice is to wait till the *Azan* (Islamic prayer call) is heard. At some places, eating with hand is preferred while fork is preferred in other places. The world population is diverse, and so are the dining cultures around the world.

If you are at a party where everyone uses a fork and see one person eating with his fingers, do not make fun of him. Respect the diversity. If certain kind of food is prohibited at some places, follow the rule. Non-veg food is banned in a few hotels, while alcohol is banned in many other hotels and functions. As a multicultural world, we must be able to appreciate and respect diverse dining cultures. Nor should we ever attempt judging any particular dining culture with the yardsticks of another. Cultures vary and so vary the yardsticks.

Enjoy every bite while you eat. Feel the taste on your tongue. Show respect and openness to those who dine with you, and most importantly, do not waste food. Even if it is a buffet dinner, no need to take all the dishes in the first serve, you can help yourself multiple times. Do not be that awkward guy carrying a hill in your palm!

> "Good manners are just a way of showing other people that we have respect for them."
>
> - Bill Kelly

Now, have you ever judged anyone's dining culture as inferior or untidy? Or have you ever been ridiculed for your dining culture? Yes, or no, the fact is as simple as this; No dining culture is superior or inferior in any sense. Some of them may appear to be inferior or superior, because you tend to judge a culture with the yardsticks of another one. Calculating distance in kilograms is a dumb act. Isn't it?

> "Dining is a culture-specific art. It commands respect, not judgment."
>
> - Muneer Amayoor

67 TURN YOUR PASSION INTO CASH

There was nothing unusual about the morning. As usual, millions of people woke up from their sleep, so did the birds and animals and everyone went out seeking their daily share of bread. But, not for the fourteen-year old Ramsheed from Nilambur in Kerala. He woke up from the sleep, with his whole body shaking feverishly and a high temperature. Every moment, a cold wave ran all over his body, it made his body shake like a leaf. He felt tired like never before and he could not move his legs back or forth. He felt as if his legs were completely paralysed. Anxious and worried, his mother rushed him to a hospital.

"It seems like everything is not quite right with the kidneys."

Said the doctor, as sympathetically as he can. In the next few hours, Ramsheed was run through a number of diagnostic procedures and tests. With each test, frightened about the worst that may come, his heart was pounding and so was his mother's.

After examining the scan report, the doctor called him and his mother to the doctor's cabin.

"Both the kidneys have failed. He won't last long without an immediate transplantation", said the doctor barely able to look into their eyes.

For Ramsheed, it felt that the doctor's each word weighed a million pounds and he felt as if he was being crushed underneath them. His father had passed away years ago and he was raised by his mother who supported the family by working as a maidservant in several households in the neighbourhood. They were already struggling hard to make both ends meet and they had nothing much set aside as savings. Ramsheed and his mother felt helpless. However, kind hearts came forward, donating every little sum to help the desperate family and the transplantation was successfully carried out on time.

If any of your friends or relatives happens to be a kidney patient, you might know how expensive the post-transplantation medication is. Regular medicines to be taken after the transplantation were forbiddingly expensive for Ramsheed's family. It was at this point Ramsheed himself found a way to meet the expenses. This time, surprisingly, his hobbies came to his aid.

Ramsheed was extremely fond of history. His hobbies included philately, numismatics and a huge collection of antics and archaeologically important pieces. He decided to convert his passion into profit. His collection of stamps boasted of stamps from almost every country on the planet. Equally huge was his coin and currency collection. Furthermore, he sought help from his friends, relatives and teachers to collect more items to enrich his collection.

Later, he started conducting exhibitions in schools and colleges where his collections were much appreciated. Ramsheed did not drop his studies, instead, he took leave on certain days for exhibition. One of his collections was an Olympic Medal, which none of his visitors had ever seen. Most of the students had never heard of some of the early electronic and non-electronic equipments that were on show. Besides, unlike visiting a regular museum where absolute silence is maintained, Ramsheed narrated the story behind every piece that was on show. The impressed visitors gifted him money, some in large amounts, some in little amounts they could afford and Ramsheed was finally able to make enough money for his monthly medication expenses. Apart from the pure educational experience that his exhibitions offered, his own story inspired many students in various ways.

Now, with the income from the exhibitions, Ramsheed is able to meet his monthly medical expenses. And he does all these, without dropping his studies. Ramsheed, surely, is a stubborn young boy whose life is an incredible story of resilience and indomitable spirit. He is a warrior. I had found his story, genuinely inspiring that once I featured him on my show "Blooming Dreams" at All India Radio. It still remains one of the best episodes I ever made.

> **"The weak fall, but the strong will remain and never go under!"**
>
> **- Anne Frank**

Any moment, your life could be turned upside down. Accept the insecurities of life and be brave to fight any odds that might be hurled at you.

> **"When you are locked down, it is time to break through, not to break up."**
>
> **- Muneer Amayoor**

68 NEVER MAKE MONEY

Apart from the clothes covering your dead body, what else can you take to your grave when you die? NOTHING!

You could die any moment in your life. I could die even before finishing this sentence. With your death, everything comes to a halt. The wealth you earned so hard will not follow you to the grave.

Let me tell you a short story now.

"I'll make a deal with you. Run....Run in a circle and the whole land you cover, will be all yours. The bigger your circle, the more land you'll win"

The king made this offer to a man. But it was on one condition, the man has to complete the circle and reach the starting point before the dawn. "I'm gonna be the richest man in the village. Never thought it's that easy to get rich", the man repeated to himself as he started his run. After running for an hour, he felt tired and wanted to take rest, but he did not. "Why waste time resting? I'll lose land", the man thought to himself and increased his pace. Hours passed, his throat dried and he wanted to drink some water. He saw a pond there, but thought not to have water.You cannot run long distance if you drink in the midst of running. To cover more land, he ran as fast as he can.

By the noon time, he started to feel hungry and his legs began to give up. He wanted to have some food. A mango tree was found on the way with plenty of mangoes hanging on its low branches. He looked at the mangoes and wanted to have some. At that time, he saw a wealthy man passing by."I wanna be wealthier than him.Then I can buy the tastiest mango in the world", he continued his running. On the way, he saw an old man asking for help to get up from his seat. He did not stop there fearing that he would lose a few inches of land if he cared to help the man in need of help.

When a little more time was left for the dawn, the king and his team were waiting at the starting point. They saw the man limping towards them. It appeared that his legs were giving away and he was hardly able to stand upright. His clothes were socked in his sweat. His eyes were about to close, but his lips were moving, saying "My land.. my land..". When he was just a feet away from the finishing point, his eyes rolled back, his parched lips ceased moving, he felt dizzy, his legs gave up and he collapsed to the ground. "Water, water.." he groaned. His chest expanded and shrank with a long breath. His eyes were closed. He spoke no more.

"Now, he needs just six foot of land", one man commented from the crowd.

If you run behind money, you will have to sacrifice your comfort, peace of mind, love, relationships, values and much more. At the same time, if you run behind your passion, doing what you love, money will follow you. It will bring all the comfort you need. Unlike the man in the story, you can take your last breath, peacefully, surrounded by your loved ones.

> **"That man is richest whose pleasures are cheapest".**
>
> **– Henry David Thoreau**

Please don't get me wrong. I don't mean to say that earning money is bad. It is not. Instead, I want to remind you that money is not all that matters. The purpose behind earning the money matters too. After all, you cannot take your wealth to your grave. That means, the purpose behind earning money should go beyond your narrow self interests.

Ask yourself,

- How will my business help people improve the quality of their life?
- How will the online course I offer transform the lives of other people?
- How will my farm produce nourish the consumer's health?
- How will my wealth benefit my fellow beings?
- How will my knowledge benefit the children in my neighbourhood?

Put your endeavours in the bigger perspective. When the purpose is inspiring, you get an avalanche of energy within. Every penny that you earn becomes more meaningful. Make money, enjoy abundance, feel the joy of giving, and experience the power of empowering others with your wealth, health and mind. What counts at the end of your life is not how much money you have earned, but how many lives you have transformed.

> "Money is meaningful only if you know why you are earning it."
>
> - Muneer Amayoor

69 PROMISE LESS, DELIVER MORE!

My brother, Mubarak's house is under construction now. You know, with appointments with engineers, ordering construction materials, coordinating the whole work and running never-ending errands, it is a busy time for him. For the masonry works, he ordered ten loads of bricks, with each load containing 250 bricks. The price per brick was decided to be at ₹ 42. However, when the first load arrived, just out of curiosity, my brother counted the bricks. Instead of 250 bricks, there were a total of 255 bricks. That means, five extra bricks were delivered. We were amused and when we asked about it, the owner of the quarry told that it was their custom. Every load comes with extra five bricks.

"That's how we do it. You know, some bricks may get damaged while transporting. We try to make up for that. That's all."

We were moved by the honesty he keeps in his business. When we talked to the mason we had hired, he said that, in the worst case, only one or two bricks will be damaged during the transportation.

Not much. Yet, the quarry owner delivers five extra bricks with every load. However, customers have to pay only for 250 bricks and they would deliver 255 bricks. In effect, when the whole ten loads were delivered, we got extra 30 bricks for free.

Apart from being moved by the quarry owner's honesty, it set me thinking. I did some calculations. You see, when he delivers 100 loads of bricks, he is giving away a huge profit of 500 bricks that would make 2 loads. The sacrifice that he makes to keep his honesty in the business is a model for any entrepreneur to follow. Instead of incurring loss, it could even increase his customer base. Do you know why? When heard about it, one of my relatives who was looking for ordering bricks for his own house construction did not waste any second to contact the same quarry owner.

The business model is not only honest; it is sustainable, profitable and keeps his customers super happy. You can use this tactic in any area to ensure that your customer is not just satisfied, but delighted. Give something extra. Go an extra mile to delight your customer.

> "There is a big difference between a satisfied customer and a loyal customer. Never settle for 'satisfied'."
>
> – Shep Hyken

What you give extra, matters. Remember, more than anything else, a delighted customer is your best advertisement.

> "Delight people with your service, because satisfaction is for mediocre."
>
> \- Muneer Amayoor

70 ORDER IN CHAOS

Four or five tiny egg-puffs up against several hungry young men in their prime. In a matter of few seconds, the poor puffs were ripped into tiny little pieces that suddenly disappeared into the young men's hungry mouth. I am talking about what happened just a few days before our college magazine release.

The date for the magazine release was already set. Magazine work was yet to finish. The magazine team was literally racing against the clock. On this particular day, we had gathered in the college hall as early as 9 in the morning and we worked late into night with little or nothing to eat. As often happens with every college magazine work, we were running short on fund. Anyway, we raised a little sum and two guys were sent to buy as many egg puffs as we can afford. The rest of us continued the work. The moment the two guys finally showed up with a white plastic bag in their hand, they were surrounded by the rest of the team. There was no time to neatly untie the bag, there was no time to count how many puffs were in there, there was no time to cut them into equal pieces. Instead all the hell was broken loose and in a split-second the plastic bag was ripped into pieces. In an instant, nothing was left in the bag. When the bag was empty, we grabbed pieces from each other's hands. It was all chaotic. Yet, it spoke volumes about our friendship and its depth. Some got more, some got less, but none complained a word. There was a special joy in it. We were truly present in those moments of sheer chaos, we were together in it. Without our love and care for each other, the situation could have dissolved into a brawl. But, we understood each other. We loved each other. We cared for each other. There was an order to the chaos. The picture we clicked on that night is one of my all-time favourites and the taste of those puffs still lingers in my mouth.

When our friends are around, every little thing turn into a celebration. No matter where you are, a five-star hotel or a wayside makeshift restaurant, time spent with your friends is joyous like no other time.

> **"A single rose can be my garden... a single friend, my world."**
>
> **– Leo Buscaglia**

Life is busy. It is also incredibly short. Can you find some time out of your schedule to laugh with your friends and share love with each other?

> "Laugh with your friends, live with a smile, love with your heart."
>
> - Muneer Amayoor

71 STOP COMPARING NOW

Imagine a male peacock fanning out its feathers in a proud display of its beauty and elegance. Now, imagine a crow perched on a leafless branch. Both are birds and they have their own unique qualities, still, we compare and judge them based on their immediate appearance. In fact, can we compare these two birds? I would say, no. The peacock is unique when it comes to the vibrant hues of its feathers and its beauty. Does it mean that the peacocks are superior to the crows? No, absolutely no. A crow may look less appealing to your eyes, but the crows are generally more intelligent than the peacocks. Besides, crows can fly long and high-a general trait of the most birds. What about the peacocks? Can they fly as high or long as the crows? No. Does it mean that the crows are superior to peacocks? No, absolutely not. Neither are the crows superior to the peacocks, nor are the peacocks superior to the crows. They are, what they are, and they are beautiful the way they are. Can you compare the elephants with horses? No. The elephants are known for their intelligence and sheer strength while the horses are known for their agility and speed. You cannot compare them. You may like one of them more for your own personal reasons or you may like both of them equally. But, you cannot weigh and judge them. You cannot say one of them is better. They are what they are, and they are beautiful the way they are.

Do you ever try comparing and judging your brain and heart for the distinct functions they perform? It would be the height of the stupidity to say that "I love my heart more than my brain", or vice-versa.

In the natural world, comparison is virtually impossible and so is it when it comes to our children. Everyone is unique. If you doubt, compare your thump impression with that of your friend. Even the identical twins do not have matching finger prints. Everyone is unique, so are you and so is your child. Unique. A child prodigy in mathematics may not be great with guitar. A child who is a music sensation from the very young age may not be as talented a footballer as his neighbouring boy. A little scientist may not be good at memorising poems.

Didn't you, after all, notice that the Young Sheldon Cooper is good only in science?

Each and every child is blessed in his/her own way. Your task is not to complain that your child does not sing as good as your brother's child. Comparing your child is doing disservice to identifying his/her talents. In fact, your children are born with a unique gift-box from the Creator. Your task is to help them find the key to unlock the God-given talent-box. Once they open up the box, they will make you proud.

"Children are not things to be moulded, but are people to be unfolded" –Jess Lair

You cannot pressure your children to be a genius. But you can provide your children a conducive environment to help them take risks, make mistakes, explore themselves and identify their talents. They will do the rest. Trust them.

"Your children are unlike any other children before or after them."

- Muneer Amayoor

72 RULES MATTER, THEY DO!

The day my brother tasked me with a serious postman's job. I have a photographic memory of the day's events. I was young and my elder brother asked me to deliver an application form at Farook College, Calicut, in Kerala. Travelling by a bus, I reached the place and I had to cross a busy highway to get to the college. After ensuring that no vehicles were coming, I crossed half of the road and stood right on the divider line where it was safe. To be frank, I was a bit frightened as the highway was heavy with traffic and if you have ever been to India, you might know that we do not boast of the best driving culture in the world! Before crossing the second half of the road, I made it sure that no vehicle was close enough to hit me, before I make it to the other side. Just after taking 2-3 steps, a scooter suddenly came out of nowhere and hit me. The scooter was coming in the wrong direction after overtaking another vehicle. The scooter hit me on my thigh and threw me a couple of feet away. The next thing I remember is lying in the road right in front of a car. Luckily, it was a Police car, and the driver had managed to stop it on time. In case there was a slight delay in the drivers' response, probably, you would not be reading this book today. I am here today, thanks to his quick reflux.

Riding the scooter were two young college students, probably just as young as I was at the time. I think that they were on their way to some party or celebration. Because, both of them wore black T-shirts and one of them had a "+" sign on his shirt while the other had a "-" sign on his shirt. Luckily, apart from torn clothes, we had sustained no major injury to speak of. The fault was clearly on their side, however, I did not make a big fuss about it as I did not want them to get into trouble with a police case. They were young, just like I was. They must have felt an overdose of confidence and enthusiasm, which made them think that they can overtake easily even through the wrong side. They must have believed that they will never hit another man or vehicle since they were expert riders.

Just think, what would have happened if that police car had run over any of us? What if one of us was mortally wounded? What if one of us had legs broken? Everything can wait; there is no need to put your life at risk to reach somewhere one or two minutes early. Everyone is busy. Everyone has their own priorities as well.

Rules matter. Rules do matter. Not just while driving, rules matter in your life as well. Rules are meant to keep everyone safe and disregarding them could lead to tragedies that cannot be undone.

> "Patience is not simply the ability to wait - it's how we behave while we're waiting."
>
> \- Joyce Meyer

It's okay to be late sometimes. It's far better to reach 10 minutes late than never reaching your destination. If you think you are in a hurry, remember everyone is always in hurry. Always.

> "Driving license does not come with commonsense. You have to develop it."
>
> \- Muneer Amayoor

73 CHILDREN SEE YOU

A fine Sunday. My mother and wife were cooking something special and I was fixing my two-year old son's toy car in the kitchen. As I was trying to repair the broken toy car, pretending to be an accomplished mechanic, my little son was acting as my assistant. It was when I was looking for the knife that my eyes fell on a chocolate bar in the cupboard. "Let the mechanic's works take a pause", I thought, "let me first finish this chocolate bar". I took it in my hand and gave the first piece to my mother. Seeing this, and eager to get his share, my son burst out crying. It was too loud to bear; I gave him the rest of the chocolate. We were expecting that he would devour it in a few seconds. But, to everyone's astonishment, he did not eat it himself; instead he broke it into two and gave the first portion to his mother, my wife. Taking her portion, my wife took him up in her hand and kissed all over his face in an impatient show of love. My mother, with her teary eyes remarked, "See, he is learning from you, my son. You gave the first portion to your mother and he gave the first portion to his mother!"

"What can you do to promote world peace? Go home and love your family."

- Mother Teresa

How do you behave with your family members when your children are around? Is your behaviour an example for them to follow? Yes or no, they learn from you.

"Children do what they see, not what you say."

- Muneer Amayoor

74 LIFE IS BUT A BRIEF STINT ON THE EARTH

A thick wallet, an enormous bank balance, an apartment overlooking the ocean, an expensive summer home in the suburbs, the most advanced cars and the latest model of smartphone. Who does not have a friend or a relative whose long list of material goals keep them always on the toe? Well, it is, indeed, great to have an inspiring goal. I do not dispute that it keeps you motivated and focused. However, what if it becomes the sole purpose of your life? What if you end up devoting all day and night, chasing your material goals? If you devote 24x7 for that, the balance sheet of your life may not match up. Ask yourself, "What do you earn money for? Is it only to add more digits to your bank balance? Or, do you earn money to ensure a better quality of life?"

When we get completely lost in our pursuit for material goals, we feel always incomplete. Nothing would suffice us; we end up chasing goal after goal, possession after possession and at the end of the day life becomes a never-ending circle of desire-pursuit-goal-desire. It would instill within us, a sense that we are always, incomplete, insufficient, weak and not enough. In a pursuit for the completeness, we chase our material goals-money, luxury, cars, big apartments, reputation, prestige, fame, the list would go infinitely long. Even after securing, accomplishments after accomplishments, we feel unaccomplished. Life becomes a never-ending pursuit. Imagine a cheetah destined to spend its life chasing a deer it can never catch up with. All along, we forget to live. Close your eyes and think about it, you achieved everything possible in your life and in the death-bed, when you are about to breathe your last, you realise that all along you forgot to live.

You have a big apartment with the best view of the sunset, you have an enormous bank balance, there is that expensive luxury car of yours in the garage, the accomplishments, recognitions, awards and certificates you won are displayed in your living room and yet, you do not have any memories of any sweet moment with your spouse or children, you could not accomplish your parents' last wish and when they finally passed away, you even forgot to mourn their death. Tell me, is that life worth living? It is not. IT IS NOT.

"Your family and your love must be cultivated like a garden. Time, effort, and imagination

must be summoned constantly to keep any relationship flourishing and growing."

- Jim Rohn

At least once in a week, find a few hours to sit back, to put your feet up and listen to your favourite tracks or to meditate, laugh out loud, or just chatter with friends and family. Surviving is not living. You have only one life. It is a brief and fast stint on the earth. Live your brief stint on the earth. You have no time to postpone it.

"Live like it's the last day of your life."

- Muneer Amayoor

75 RELIVE THAT MOMENT

After getting married, my wife and I had gone for a little trip to Adyanpara waterfalls at Nilambur, Kerala. We were accompanied by my cousin and his wife as well. Upon reaching the destination, the two couples split and went in two directions. It was a truly red-letter day for both of us. We walked hand in hand by the rapids and found an ideal place for us to sit. On the one side, the mighty rapids thundered down its path and on the other side, trees and small plants thrived. In between, the nature had carved out a flat rock for us to sit and talk. With thundering water and chirruping birds as witness to our love, we sat against the backdrop of a scenic landscape with her head resting on my right shoulder. She placed her palm in mine and we kept on talking for God alone knows how long. We did not know the time passing by as we were completely oblivious to the rest of the world. It was only when the echoes of the Azan, the Muslim prayer call reached our ears, we knew how long we had spent talking to each other. Together, facing the west, we performed the evening prayer on the same rock. After the prayer, as we both turned to each other, our eyes happened to meet each other's and those shining eyes and hearty smile on her face grow dearer to me by each passing day. The air was thick with love, romance and divine presence. The landscape, love and divine presence combined to move us into tears, our eyes were wet with tears of joy and we did not notice it until it brimmed over our eyes. We thanked God, for uniting us forever.

However, when we returned to our car, a surprising twist was waiting for us. My cousin and his wife were impatiently waiting for us. They looked really upset and worried. He had called me on the phone several times, however the call was not connected since we were out of network coverage area. You might be wondering why my cousin was so worried. Apparently, a lot had happened when I and my wife were lost in ourselves. A major fight had taken place between some of the visitors and the security guards at the site. The police had arrived, and the misbehaving visitors were forcefully sent away. As I said earlier, my wife and I were totally immersed in ourselves and were oblivious to the rest of the world. One of the security members had asked my cousin to leave as early as possible, because it was no longer safe for the families to be there. However, when my cousin Salahudheen failed to contact me, he feared for our safety and was anxiously waiting for us to return. As soon as he saw us, he said,"Get in the car, we need to leave as soon as possible". All the way back home, the other couple kept on teasing us saying we were made for each other that nothing in the world mattered to us when we were together.

Nowadays, whenever I feel down, I close my eyes and recall this joyous afternoon. In fact, since I have a photographic memory of the day, each time I recall the afternoon, I am able to, literally, relive those moments of poor joy and spiritual love. Each time I feel down, the memories of that fine afternoon rejuvenate me. As almost all other couples, we also get into little fights sometimes. However, all those fights strengthen our bond. If we fight, in no time the memories of that blessed afternoon will creep into our mind and as a result, every fight would make our love stronger and more passionate. Each passing moment, we keep falling deeper in love with each other.

> "A happy moment can last a lifetime if you remember to smile when you think of it."
>
> - Anonymous

What is that one picture in your mind that can light up your mood any moment?

"Identify that one moment you had in your life which can instantly take you to a happier state, and relive that moment to relieve yourself from negativity."

- Muneer Amayoor

76 GIVE UNCONDITIONALLY

"Can I have something to eat? I am starving."

An old man, probably in his late seventies, wearing worn out mucky clothes knocked on Arya's door. With his untrimmed hair and beard covered in dust, the thin and weary old man looked pathetic in his appearance. Arya could not help pitying the old man and gave him what she had cooked for lunch. Sitting on her door step, the man gobbled up everything in his plate and Arya was dumbstruck by his appetite. The old man did not say anything when he left, but his eyes spoke volumes about his gratitude. That noon, Arya had nothing much left for her lunch as the old man had eaten up everything. She had no complaints. That afternoon, however, she slept well and could not wait for her husband to arrive to recount her delight on helping the old man.

The old man arrived on time the next day as well and soon he became a regular visitor. Arya served him happily, besides, her husband was happy about it too. Every day, he would knock on the door and sit on the doorstep for his lunch to be supplied. This continued day after day, yet they spoke no word to each other. On the days, she had gone out, she would leave the food on the doorstep and the old man would have his meal as usual.

After a couple of months, while having his lunch, the old man grumbled, "It's the worst food I ever had in my life", he lifted his face to meet her eyes and said, "Hey lady, do you cook it for me or for the dogs? It tastes terrible now. It was tasty in the first few weeks... I will give you that....But these days, it's terrible." However, he wiped his plate clean and walked away as usual. Arya was shocked by his words and countenance. Never did she think that the old man would talk like that. Lying in her bed, staring at the wall, she thought how rude and ungrateful the man was. "Never again. Never. I will never feed him again. NEVER", she thought to herself. That day, she could not take her usual afternoon nap.

When her husband came home from the work, she recounted the whole incident to him. He said, "I'm sorry to tell you this. Darling, your thoughts have spoiled your virtue. When you give someone something, never expect anything in return, not even a word of gratitude. You're doing angel's work, please do not stain your good deeds with these harsh words. I would rather have you continue your good work, than stopping it. Don't give a damn about what he says, or what others say. Just keep doing your good work, my love." The man never knew what or where would be his next meal. However, for the rest of his life, he knew where his lunch was. At Arya's.

When I was studying for B.Tech. at Munnar, my friend Nijas and I used to observe fasting in the holy month of Ramadan. Nijas was my roommate. For fasting, we would get up early in the morning at about 4 A.M. and have some food. Not much. Then, we would break the fasting at about 7 P.M. Since the climate in at the Munnar is chilling cold, it was not practical to buy cooked meal and keep it for the next morning. Besides, we were not great cooks to wake up as early as three in the morning and cook meal to start off the fasting. Our only resort was the fruits we would buy from a street vendor. Every day, I and Nijas would hit the street and buy two oranges, two apples and two mangoes. Since we used to buy fruits from the same vendor every day, he noticed us.

"People usually buy from me half a kilogram or more, none buys one or two pieces as you two do. I don't understand why....", the street vendor was curious about us.

When we told him why we did what we did, he replied with a smile, "So, that's the deal. You two are fasting...", putting a couple of extra fruits in our plastic bag, he continued, "There you go, some extra fruits for the special customers".

We insisted him to accept the cash for the extra fruits, but he would not accept. Again and again we asked him to take the cash for it, but he would not take it. We were shocked by this man's kindness. He did not know who we were, he did not even know our names, still, he was kind to us. The next day as well, the same thing repeated. No matter what we said, he would not accept the money. The same thing repeated for the whole month and my friend and I still remain indebted to him. He was not a rich man, nor was a he a business magnet. He was only a street vendor selling fruits in a small cart. He was not rich, but he had a big heart and to this day, this debt remain unpaid. We are forever indebted to him. He may have forgotten us, but we have not. For me, not a single Ramadan passes by, without remembering him. To this day, my friend and I pray for him every time we are reminded of him. We are indebted to him forever.

What is the way to repay such debts? There is only one way and that is to help other people around you, at least ten fold. Kindness can be weighed against kindness only.

"Service to others is the rent you pay for your room here on earth."

– Muhammed Ali

As social animals we all help other people and seek help from others. However, do you feel sad if someone you helped turn "ungrateful" to you? If yes, it means that your help is not unconditional, you expect gratitude in return. Giving should not be to feed your ego. It should be an unconditional act of kindness in hope of nothing in return- *Nishkam Karma.*

"Kindness can be paid back only in kind acts."

- Muneer Amayoor

77 WHEN COURAGE MEETS COMPASSION

Can you recall a daring act of courage you have done or witnessed?

The greatest acts of courage I have directly witnessed so far were in the year 2019. In the year 2019, Kerala, a small state at the southern tip of the Indian peninsula, was hit by a devastating flood of biblical proportions. In the unprecedented deluge, cities were submerged, thousands of houses were destroyed, farm fields were flooded and hundreds were killed. The whole state came into a virtual standstill. With police, fire and rescue team, quick response team, and the three forces at work, the government was doing a commendable job. However, it was not enough. Common people, government employees and even celebrities were involved in rescue works. However, nothing matched the unparalleled dedication and sheer courage shown by fishermen from different parts of the state. Putting their own life at risk and damaging their means of livelihood, the fishing boats, they saved thousands of lives. The Chief

Minister of Kerala, Mr. Pinarayi Vijayan rightly called them "Kerala's Own Army".

"Kerala's Own Army" consisted of fishermen from different parts of Kerala including Ponnani, Calicut, Kollam, Kochi, Trivandrum, Koottayi etc. They rushed to the flood hit areas to save the people.

Once the flood retrieved, I and my colleagues from the All India Radio went to Ponnani beach to prepare a radio feature on the voluntary rescue operations carried out by the fishermen. It was around 11 AM when our team reached there. Curious to see our vehicle bearing the name board and emblem of the All India Radio, the fisher folk quickly gathered around us. When we told them that we had come to feature them on AIR, they were excited.

The friendly men took us straight to a nearby hut they had made for them to sit and talk. It was a nice and small hut roofed with coconut leaves. People ranging from 20s to 60s sat in a circle and shared their heroic exploits during the flood. They had received the call from the police, requesting support in rescue operation on a Friday morning. The moment they got the call, they packed the necessary materials, and loaded the boats to trucks.

Their hard work started with loading the heavy boats to the trucks to be carried to the flood hit areas. Each boat weighed tons and they had no mechanical supports to lift them up. As it was Friday, some of them had to attend the Friday Jumua prayer. However, they skipped it and went to save lives.They understood that the best worship at the time was saving lives.

Transporting the boats itself was a challenging task as the roads were flooded.They were told that, they would get the fuel to operate the boats from the site. However, most petrol stations were flooded and they did not get the oil. However, since they had foreseen it, they had brought diesel in advance. With not enough lights, the rescue operations were especially challenging at the night.

Often the boats got stuck in the mud and salvaging operations were not easy. During the rescue operations one of the boats capsized as it hit an electric motor pump.The fishermen plunged into the muddy water, managed to stay afloat until another boat came to their rescue. They were thirsty, hungry and tired. As the supermarkets and shops were all flooded food items were in short supply. When one of the native men offered them some food, it tasted like the best food in the world.

The rescue operation continued for many days. In many flooded houses people were stuck on their roof and upstairs. The brave fishermen had to dive in the muddy water to even find the way inside the house, once in, they helped people to get onboard and hurried them to safety. In one of the houses, they saw an elderly couple lying on a table surrounded by water. If the rescue team was a bit late both of them would have drowned to death. Rescuing pregnant women, children, elderly people and even bed-ridden patients, they saved many lives.

Nobody dared going to the areas the fishermen went bravely. Once an officer got onboard their boat, as he wanted to examine the situation. However, just after a few minutes, the roaring water started to toss the boat up and down. The poor officer screamed,"Please take me to the land, I will die here."The fishermen replied, "Sir, if we live, you too will live, if we die in this water, you too will, be brave."

They risked their lives, and saved thousands of people. They expected nothing in return, not even a word of gratitude. We talked for hours together. What we saw there, was hard for our hearts to bear. These fishermen and women live in huts that leak in the rainy season and hunger is a regular visitor for them. However, they were rich in love and compassion for their fellow men. They knew what it means to have your houses flooded, they knew what it means to go hungry and they knew what the people of Kerala were going through during the flood. They mustered up all their courage and put their own life in arms way, so that thousands could survive a devastating flood. Their pain, their hunger and their knowledge that, as fishermen, their life is at the mercy of nature, push them to love one another embrace humanity.

"Goodness is love in action."

- James Hamilton

Have you ever saved anyone's life? Will you risk your life to save a stranger?

"Greatest heroes do not have superpowers; they live right among us and spring up to action when the situation demands it."

- Muneer Amayoor

78 ARE YOU THAT FROG?

My friend, Maqsood used to work as a teacher, in Male', the capital city of Maldives, a beautiful and small island nation in the middle of the Indian Ocean. Geographically, Maldives is an archipelago of a few tiny islands. During the free time, talking with his students was a hobby for him. He was particularly interested in talking to the students from the tiny remote islands. Unlike the regular students from the capital city, these students had lived most of their life only on their little islands. Before they came to the capital for their studies, they had never left their little islands. They did not know much about where and how other people lived. To make it worse, during their childhood days, TV networks were not common on their islands. In effect, you could say that these kids lived most of their life cut off from the rest of the world. Their tiny little island was their world, it was their universe. Their horizon was limited to these small islands surrounded by the blue sea. A small stretch of land, whichever direction they look, they could see only the sea. No hills, no mountains, and no large landmasses. A small stretch of land surrounded by the sea.

"Dear ones, the world is so vast. You should go out and see the world around."

"What do you mean? Vast? Vast like what?", one of the students asked.

"Vast, really vast. Unlike these beautiful little islands, the continents are so vast that you cannot even see where the land ends.", he continued.

"You are kidding, sir. There can't be land like that. There has to be the sea around, right?" a student voiced her confusion. These students had lived all their life only on the little islands and they couldn't comprehend the idea of the land being vast. They asked many questions.

As a last resort to explain the idea, he illustrated the example of his own country, India, the seventh largest country in the world.

"In India, if you take a train from the southern end of the country to the northern end, it will take you 3-4 days to reach there. That's how big India is.", he tried his best to explain.

But it did not quite work. One of the students commented, "Sir, you need to change your trains, they are too slow". The girl who had lived her entire life on a tiny island surrounded by the sea, could not comprehend the vastness of the world. The little world of the small island was everything for her. Her horizon was limited to it.

Leave the little girl, do not judge her, one day, she would definitely understand how large the world is, and she would travel everywhere. Here I am trying to talk about another class of people who remain ignorant and closed by their choice.

Some people are like a frog in a little pond. A frog that refuses to step out of the little pond. Such people think that the pond is the whole world. They have never cared to look beyond their little pond and think that they know everything there is to know about the world. For them, the water in the pond, little fish and insects in the pond, that is all they have seen.

The trouble is when they judge everything based on their limited knowledge. You cannot defeat them by arguing. You could not apply logic if you argue with them. Because their little world defies all the logic, they live in a parallel universe where general principles of commonsense and logic cannot be applied. If your supervisor or boss is of such personality, you will have a hard time convincing him/her about anything. Your creative ideas will never be accepted. What's the way out then?

There is only one way to help such people. Push them out of their little bubble. Take that frog out of the pond and let it see the world beyond. Unless they are forced out, they will keep imposing their unreliable judgments on the rest.

> "No matter where you go or what you do, you live your entire life within the confines of your head."
>
> - Terry Josephson

Never let yourself be confined to your little world. Always, try to push your boundaries; try to explore the world beyond the confines of your little world. The more you explore, the more you will understand. The more you understand, the more humble you will become.

> "When you break the invisible wall around your thoughts, you will be able to liberate yourself."
>
> - Muneer Amayoor

79 WHY? THE REASON TO BE

What is the purpose of your life? Think for a while before you read on.

Burning midnight's oil, preparing for the upcoming entrance test. Racing against the clock to catch up with the deadlines. Scheduling new appointments to further your business interests. Sleepless nights spent brainstorming for new business ideas. Digging through the journals and articles to stay updated in your field. All of us can identify with some of these pursuits. But, how many of us do really pose to reflect "why?" How many of us really ask ourselves, "Why am I in this pursuit?" What do you hope to find at the end? Where do you hope to reach at the end? Is it to become a millionaire, or to have more acceptance in the society or to wield more power or is it simply to get fame? You can have any of these or all of these as your goal. But there has to be a transcending purpose as a motivation for your pursuits.

Here, I do not use the word purpose in its usual sense. Your purpose should be something that transcends your aim and goal. It should be something that transcends yourself. It should have nothing to do with you as an individual. To set a purpose for your efforts, ask yourself, "In what way, my efforts are going to benefit others?" The answer to this question should be the PURPOSE behind your efforts.

In other words, if you invest your time, money and energy to pursue a particular course, define, how that course will help others, once you graduate. Before you pursue something, clearly define, how your pursuit can add value to the lives of people around you. That, essentially means, your pursuit does not end once you reach your goal. Your goal is only a stepping stone to help you fulfil your purpose.

For example, if your mission is to become a doctor, say, an Oncologist, your purpose should sound like as follows:

"I want to become an Oncologist and through my service, I want to help cancer patients relieve their pain and enable them to live healthy and happy life after their recovery. If they are terminally ill, I want to enable them, at least to live a reasonably dignified life until they die"

This means that your goal is not an end in itself. Your pursuit does not come to an end simply by becoming an Oncologist. Becoming an Oncologist is only a stepping stone to fulfil the WHY-QUESTION which fuels your pursuit. This is not to mean that you are not supposed to have any other desires. It is perfectly OK for you to wish to become a millionaire, or to desire fame, or whatever you wish for as long as they do not override your purpose.

A clear and well-defined purpose is a prerequisite to lead a happy and content life. Ask yourself, what your purpose is. Your purpose is not what you want to be. Your purpose is what you want to do once you become what you want to be. What changes do you hope to bring to the life of others once you reach your goal. Your purpose does not have an end as it is an infinite task and it is exactly this infinite nature of your purpose that should keep you going. Your purpose is why you keep going.

If you do not have a visionary purpose, once you achieve your goal, you will feel that everything is done. "I have nothing else to do now. I can take rest", not only this thought would make your life monotonously boring. It can also make your life appear meaningless and not worth living. What more do you need to harbour suicide thoughts in your mind?

"The only thing worse than being blind is having sight but no vision."

- Helen Keller

A strong mission keeps you focused while a strong purpose keeps you motivated all the time.

"Your Purpose is why you are."

- Muneer Amayoor

80 THE SWEET ARBITRATOR

When I look back at my younger self, often it occurs to me that I used to be a practicing Gandhi when I was a little boy. Weird thing is that it was even before I knew who Gandhi, actually, was.

You might have heard about Gandhian mode of protests called Satyagraha and how it helped India in its fight against the British colonial oppression. Recently, it became clear to me that I was actually practicing one of Gandhian Satyagrahas called Hunger Strike and that too, long before I had come to learn about it. Gandhi used to go on Hunger Strike as a means of protesting against certain oppressive laws. And most times, his protests did not go unnoticed. Now, I remember my fasting strikes in my childhood days! Yes, after making some silly issues at home or after getting scolded by my mom or dad, I would announce my hunger strike. I would throw myself in the bed without eating anything. Hunger would often tempt me to get up and call off the strike. Often, the aroma of the dish being cooked in the kitchen, would make me question the worth of the strike I was on. Often,

I would wonder if I had started something I could not finish! But, you know, Satyagraha is all about the power of your mind. It is all about forcing your enemy to change their mind through your will-power. Besides, it is a matter of your self-respect, right? To keep going with the strike or not? That was the question.

None of my hunger strikes were voluntarily called off by me. I was deeply loyal to the Gandhian principles! I would lie in the bed waiting for the arbitrator to come and negotiate on my behalf and I did have loyal arbitrator who would show up on time.

The arbitrator was none other than my mom, my loving mom. She would show up at my door and clear her throat to attract my attention. Then she would look into my eyes and with all the affection in the world she would take me to the dining table. On the days of hunger strikes, she would serve me some special delicacies as well! In that way my strike would be called off only to be announced again another silly day!

> "When you are looking at your mother, you are looking at the purest love you will ever know"
>
> –Charley Benetto

When was the last time you hugged your mom? When will be the next time you hug your mom?

> "Mother is the best arbitrator in the world."
>
> - Muneer Amayoor

81 WHAT DO THE HENS TEACH US?

One of the first lessons I learned about birds when I was a child was that, never get too close to a hen when she is accompanied by her newly hatched off-springs. You might have already guessed how I learned this lesson. She is always on guard and would never let anyone come close to her off-springs. No matter how big you are, if you pose a threat to her off-springs, you are nothing, but a threat and she will make you run for your life. If she spots any crows or eagles that might pose a threat to the chicks, she would immediately spread her wings and the chicks will be safe under her protective wings. How protective!

Now, if you have observed the hens, you might have noticed that their attitude towards the chicks will go a drastic change as they grow. When the chicks have grown enough to take care of themselves, the same protective mother would poke them with her beak and make them run away from her. She has done her part and now it is time for the chicks to live on their own. During the first few weeks, when the chicks were vulnerable, she gave them protection, taught them how to find food, and how to guard themselves. She taught them how to survive and how to live and now the chicks should live using the lessons their mother has taught them. Lesson-time is over, now it is time to use the lessons to make their own living. By poking, she is reminding the chicks that they cannot hide under their mother's wings forever. They have to fend for themselves.

What about humans? What about you and your children? Do you make your children hide under your wings even when they are fully grown? Your duty as a parent is not to give your children a good life when they grow up. Instead, your duty is to teach them how to make a good living when they grow up. You will not be here forever to protect them. For example, teach your child how to fish and he/she will survive, no matter what happens. If you give your children the lessons about one's own responsibilities, give them wings of hope and challenging platforms, you will witness them conquer great heights.

"If you have never been hated by your child, you have never been a parent."

- Bette Davis

What type of a parent are you? Dominating one? Over-protective one? Or motivating one? What are the changes you have to make in yourself to make yourself more of a motivating parent?

> "Teach your children the art of survival and self-sustenance."
>
> - Muneer Amayoor

82 WHAT THE PHOTOS TALK ABOUT

"I couldn't stop laughing bro....I was searching for a document and all of a sudden, there it was....that old picture of yours...ha ha.. The one we clicked in our first ever tour..... Don't you remember?.... oh man, you must see that look on your face, that funny hairstyle...oh man I laughed my head off..."

Did you ever have similar experience? For some urgent purpose, you are going through that maze of folders in your laptop, and you stumble upon one of those old pictures of yours or your friends and the next moment, you have the laugh of your life! It happens. And you forget what you were exactly looking for and get yourself lost in the old photos and the memories they have captured.

What photos do is that they immortalise an otherwise fleeting moment and every time you see them, they send you back in time. By capturing a fleeting moment for ever, every photo tells a story. A photo is a time machine that allows you to go back in time-to your childhood days, to your school days, to your college days, to your wedding day...What a beautiful feeling to get lost in our memories, good, bad and ugly.

Sometimes, when I feel down, I take a tour through my memories by going through the old photos. It's a nice feeling. However, I regret that during my school days I was so camera-shy and in none of my school pictures I look great. I look awkward.

Whenever you go outing, make it a point to click a picture that captures the moment in the best manner possible. With smartphones in our hand, clicking pictures have become easier than never before. And importantly, try not to be camera-shy. You don't want yourself to look at your old pictures and see those awkward pictures. I know the feeling. But note that camera should not get in the way of your enjoyment. However, if you pose for a pic with every step you take, when you see those pictures after long years, you will not have much of memories to get lost in. Take pictures to capture a moment, not to lose it.

> "Sometimes you will never know the value of a moment until it becomes a memory."
>
> – Dr.Seuss

Have you seen your grandparents? Do you know how they looked like when they were young like you? Weren't they just as cool as you? They were, but you never got to see that. Let your children and grandchildren know that they had cool parents and grandparents. For that, digitalise your family portraits and photo albums. Do it before those photos and negatives are irreversibly destroyed.

> "Memories offer you a beautiful hide-out."
> - Muneer Amayoor

83 UNITED LITTLE STEPS

Do you use Wikipedia? Who doesn't, right? But, have you ever thought about who is operating Wikipedia? Well, the world's largest and most comprehensive encyclopaedia cannot be operated by a single person, that is for sure. Then who is it? As far as the content is concerned, millions of people from various parts of the globe contribute content that make up the Wikipedia entries on various subjects. Once the content is created, it is edited and verified by another huge group of people who work tirelessly to make the entry better. Thus, the Wikipedia is at your service. When everyone unites making their little contributions, a giant encyclopaedia is born. Then you might wonder who is funding this expensive endeavour. Well, the mammoth fund required for its maintenance and operations is found through crowd funding. Just like millions of nameless people who create content for the Wikipedia, similar group of nameless people fund its operation as well.

Perched on the top branch of the tallest tree in the woods, the little sparrow surveyed the scenario. It was the most tragic. A hellish wildfire has broken loose, engulfing large swaths of land in the forest and it is headed for what is left of the forest. Reducing three fourth of the forest to ashes, thousands of birds and animals have already perished and with them their habitat. The little sparrow can no longer stand the devastating impact of the fire and decided to do what she can to douse the fire. She flew to a nearby pond, collected a drop of water in her beak and poured it on the ravaging fire. She repeated her daring task over and over. Seeing the little sparrow's brave act, the arrogant fire ridiculed her:

"Seriously!? Do you really think than you can beat me with these little drops of water? You gotta be kidding me...haha."

The little sparrow gave a penetrating look and replied:

"Hey you haughty fire... You better not be so contemptuous!! You know what, if every bird, animal and other living creatures pour little drops of water on you, just as I am doing now, you won't stand a chance.....Instead of fire, we will have flood here. Flood, do you hear me, flood, F-L-O-O-D"

Now, tell me, what do you think about the little sparrow's words? Isn't she right? Look at the rain, for example. After all, isn't it just a bunch of individual drops acting in unison? The little drops of water, when they act in unison, they could conjure up a torrential rain that could flood entire cities and neighbourhoods. Now, take a look at the Wikipedia, isn't it the result of little efforts by many people? Think, how a pandemic is dealt with. Everyone ranging from ministers to laymen play their own role in containing the spread of virus. Doctors and nurses spend countless hours treating the patients, people in the streets follow the preventive guidelines, NGOs offer voluntary works and financial support and the bureaucrats run the system. This is the only way we can beat any pandemic.

One uniquely quintessential quality of humans as a species is our ability to cooperate with thousands of people- both familiar and strange people. It is one of our lone distinctions, and it exactly for the same reason no monkeys were ever able to make a structure as impressive as the Pyramid or the Great Wall of China or even the modern economic system. We can trust each other and cooperate with each other and thereby accomplish great feats that are otherwise impossible. We live in the age of crowd sourcing and crowd funding. When people offer their skills and resources for accomplishing inspiring projects, it is an example for crowd sourcing. With our ability to communicate and cooperate, we coordinate volunteers willing to support a noble project. For some projects, often the fund is raised through crowd funding. The donation can be as small as a dollar or thousands of dollars. Assume, if ten thousand people donate just one dollar each, we would be able to raise a total of ten thousand dollars.

> **"If everyone is moving forward together, then success takes care of itself."**
>
> **- Henry Ford**

Little steps by many people, when effectively coordinated can move even heaven and earth. It could revolutionise noble projects and ideas.

> **"There is strength in numbers. But, only when coordinated"**
>
> **- Muneer Amayoor**

84 WORK + STUDY

When I met Ranjith for the first time, he was only a student and yet the impact he had made on me, was profound. When I was working as a Skill Development Executive for a government project in Kerala, India, he happened to be one of my students. The skill development programme that was usually conducted on off days was meant only for the senior secondary students like Ranjith. However, after a few sessions on working days as well as off days, I noted that Ranjith was regularly absent from holiday classes. Though he was a bit shy and not very talkative, he had taken his studies seriously, I had noted that earlier. Naturally, his absence was often felt.

At first, I thought that he must be playing hooky. Later, when I asked him personally, the truth was revealed.

"Sir, I'm working along with my studies. Now I'm working as a trainee in a vehicle workshop. I've to go there on holidays. They would give me ₹ 100 per day. Besides, I get to master a job", he said. With the little earnings he made, he wanted to support his family too. Once he becomes a good mechanic, he thought to himself, he would get paid well enough and he will be able to support his higher studies as well.

I felt a deep sense of respect for him. I guaranteed him that I would support him in the best way possible, so that he could make up for the lost classes and score well. He was happy and I permitted him to take leave when he needed to go to work.

As I had understood his situation and as he was enthusiastic about his studies, a good chemistry worked out between us. By the end of the year, through our partnership, I could make him a smart and energetic guy. Gradually, he dropped his shy self and started to participate in all the activities that we performed in the class. As the icing on the cake, he scored well in the exam too. Meantime, by the end of the year he had become a good bike mechanic as well.

As far as I am concerned, those students who manage to study, while supporting their family are real gems. I have also come across several other students who work, so that they could earn enough to pay their hostel fee and such. When I was doing my PG, I too used to work part time. I was working as a Skill Development Executive at that time.

Work and study.That is a beautiful combination. Some cultures, especially the western culture, welcomes the idea of combining work with studies. Meantime, South Asian culture, in general, does not welcome the idea. However, I am of the opinion that part-time work among the students must be promoted. Let them learn the value of money, and the art of earning and spending it wisely. Let them appreciate the dignity of every job and feel respect to everyone around them.

> "There is no worse material poverty, I am keen to stress, than the poverty which prevents people from earning their bread and deprives them of the dignity of work."
>
> – Pope Francis

If you are a student reading this chapter, go, find a part time work that you can do along with your course. If you are a teacher or parent, appreciate your children who manage to work while studying and motivate everyone to follow that suite.

> "A student who knows the dignity of work, grows up to become a gentle man who values everything and everyone."
>
> - Muneer Amayoor

85 WHAT WAS HIS NAME?

Imagine, you and your wife are having a fight and you two have just been invited to a special party meant only for you two. At the party, how awkward would it be!

Well, the same was about to happen to me and my wife once. For some silly reasons I cannot remember now, I fell out with my wife and refused to talk to her for a while. It was during the first few months after our marriage, a very romantic period. You know, little fights and fall outs are a part of the post-nuptial courtship! However, during the time, we got invitation for a special party at my cousin's. It was a special party for the newlyweds- me and my wife. To avoid acting awkward at the party, I decided that we should have a talk first. I was riding my motor bike, with Suhra behind me. Just to make sure that we get a relaxed ride so that we can talk on the way, I took a road through the outskirts of the town. The road snaked through a remote area and on its both sides were a wide stretch of paddy fields. In the cold breeze and the scenic beauty that surrounded us, our little fight dissolved into the thin air.

After a short while, the bike showed some trouble and came to a grinding halt. I tried to kick start the bike but to no avail. Slowly, I realised what was wrong. As a matter of fact, nothing was wrong with the bike and it was my fault. The petrol tank was virtually empty and there was no way we could restart it. Clueless about what to do next, Suhra and I stood there on the road side. It was getting late for the party and we were stuck midway through. The nearest petrol station was around 18 kilometers away and we did not have enough petrol to move even a meter. Moreover, my concern was, what I would tell my cousin if we get there late? As I said earlier, the party was exclusively for us two.

Being a remote area, there was no taxi or auto-rikshaw for us to hire. To make it worse, no network signal was available. In effect, we were stranded midway to the party. It was at that time a young biker was passing by. Sensing that something was not quite right, he stopped by.

"What's wrong brother?", he asked. I told him that we ran out of fuel.

"Don't worry, I'll give you enough petrol for you. I've plenty in my bike."

Then we were hit by another problem, to collect petrol from his fuel tank, a bottle was needed and we had none. We looked for an empty bottle everywhere in the roadside, but we could not find one. Not far from the road, there was a house and I walked towards that house in hope of getting one from there. The other man was still searching for an empty bottle in the bushes.

"Come back, I got one."The young biker saved our day.

As I was not much of a mechanic, the young man took care of everything. He disconnected the fuel pipe and collected petrol in the bottle. Then, he poured it into my fuel tank. It was more than half a litre. Then he asked me to try starting the bike. Yes! It started! Suhra and I heaved a sigh of relief.

I thanked him, but he said it was not a big deal for him. I extended a fifty rupees note, as the price of the fuel. He refused to accept it. "No, No, no cash, brother, we are humans, everyone will need help at some point of time.. take it easy..".

What was his name? Where he was going to? How was his financial condition? To this day, I know nothing about the man. It seems he didn't want us to remember him. Was he an angel God sent to help us?

Never lose your faith in humanity. Every once in a while, someone comes by to restore and reinforce our faith in humanity. It could be your friends. It could be complete strangers.

> "If a man be gracious and courteous to strangers, it shows he is a citizen of the world."
> - Francis Bacon

Did you ever have a similar experience? Yes or no, do you have a mind open enough to help a complete stranger in distress?

> "What is a little act of kindness for you could make someone else's day"
> - Muneer Amayoor

86 LET THEM FLY

“Mommy, I don’t like it here...I wanna come with you”, I would say.

“Yes of course you can. See that rocking-horse over there....Let me seat you on it... You can ride it to reach my school while I walk. Let’s see who reaches first.”

My mother would try her own tricks to keep me at my preschool while she would go to the school where she worked. Being a teacher, she did have a couple of effective trick up her sleeves.

Let me tell you, a couple of times, I did fall for this trick. Guess what, I never reached the school. Don’t get me wrong, my mom was not happy about it either. The parting time was tough for both of us. If you wonder what I am talking about, I am talking about my tryst with preschool.

If you ask me to name the place I would never want to visit again, without any hesitation, I would say it is my preschool. Sorry if I sound rude. But, truth be told, I dread at the thought of my preschool experience. At the same time, preschool is that one place most people would say they miss the most. Indeed, the general picture we have about any preschool is that, it is a kids' paradise, where every kid is free to be whatever they want to be. But, not for me! For me, however, when I think of my preschool days, the first picture that pops up in my mind is that of me sitting next to the window with tears flowing down my cheek and looking out through the window for my mom to come and pick me.

Some parents seem to think that the preschool with the most number of toys would give their kids just the environment that they need the most. In fact, at least for me, it was far from being true. On her way to the school, my mother who was a school teacher would drop me at my preschool and spend a few minutes with me before saying goodbye. The moment she left, I would burst crying. I may have had some good experiences at the preschool, but mostly, it made me miserable. From my experience and the way many preschools functions, I think, we should reconsider our preschool practices.

Firstly, preschools do not have to be a must that every kid should necessarily go through. I do not forget the fact that preschools do help kids in developing their cognitive and social abilities. Despite the benefits preschools offer, for some kids, as it was for me, preschool could also be a torture that could leave a lasting scar in their mind. Secondly, toys do not make a good preschool. At the end of the day, what matters is the environment we provide to our kids. A preschool should not act as a juvenile prison where the children's freedom is heavily curtailed. From my preschool I heard considerably more "NO"s and incredibly less "YES"s. No wonder why the little me did not like it there. Thirdly, preschools must give equal importance to the kids cognitive, mental, social, motor and creative skills. Unequal importance given to these abilities could be disastrous for kid's development. Additionally, in an environment where the kids are allowed to fly around like butterflies in a garden, they are more likely to stumble upon their best talents. What better service could a preschool provide, than helping parents identify their kids' innate talents prior to the school? Let them run around, let them make loud bursts of noise, let them get lost in the colours, let them feel that they belong here, let them find themselves.

> "The best way to make children good is to make them happy."
>
> - Oscar Wilde

The learning should take place through interactions, games and even little quarrels they make. Prisons do not make a kid better.

> "Gift your kids the wings to fly like a butterfly."
> - Muneer Amayoor

87 THOSE THREE SYLLABLES OF LOVE

"Hi all…What's up?…. A cool idea struck me yesterday… I would love to send a kissing emoji to my wife every thirty minutes…. Any app available for that? Pls comment or DM me."

So read a post on James' wall on Facebook. He was genuine about it.

"Don't worry bro… DM me her WhatsApp number, I shall take care of it", commented a guy. But, who cares to respond to every harsh comment of the FB, right?

When was the last time you genuinely and unequivocally expressed your love for your spouse? Why do some people feel that expressing their love is a silly act reserved only for the "flirting" couples or newly-weds? Expressing your love, kissing your spouse, acknowledging/complimenting your partner for something is not a sign of weakness. These simple gestures of love are actually the chain that tightens your bond. Who knows you the best? Your spouse! None else.

A word of compliment or love from his/her part would make your day.

"Today's meal...It was great, my love". "This is the best gift I ever got in my life." "I love you." "I am proud of you, my sweet heart."These sentences are short, but they could light up your spouse's day. No matter how slow you deliver your sentence, these sentences will not take half a minute to deliver. But, they could make a huge difference. Just a couple of syllables that can do wonders in your marital life.

A gesture of love, a word of acknowledgement, a hug and a kiss. These are what fuel a truly positive relationship. When you are away, do find time to text or call your spouse. Just show him/her, how much you care. Make genuine efforts to be together and celebrate special occasions.

> "When you stop expecting people to be perfect, you can like them for who they are."
>
> - Donald Miller

When will be the next time you kiss your spouse? If not now, when? When he/she is dead and gone? Remember, only time that is real is NOW, next moment does not exist yet, tomorrow does not exist yet and you don't know for sure if you would breathe your last now. Love and show your love.

> "Compliments do wonders in relationships."
> - Muneer Amayoor

88 RESPECT DIVERSITY

After almost a day's tedious work, Ram and his colleagues were dining in their office. Most days, it is the only time of the day when they could actually look at each other and have a casual talk while sharing each other's food. Usually, it is Anjana who brings most delicacies, while curry chicken cooked by Rahman's mother is everyone's favourite. However, the best day for the crew, is when John brings his spicy and mouth-watering mango pickle.

One day, Rahman brought chicken fry for all of them, making everyone go crazy; however Ram, looking at the chicken fry, said, "Sorry, I couldn't accept it today. I have decided to go on a pilgrimage in a few weeks. At this time, I am not supposed to eat from outside." Others agreed happily without taking any offence. At the same time, they accepted the dishes that Ram brought.

Our cultures and values vary from place to place, from religion to religion and from person to person. It is, precisely, this diversity that makes us beautiful. Imagine a garden with only one kind of flowers. How plain and unappealing it would be? Our society is like a beautiful garden dotted with multifavious flowers of diverse hues and shades. Our beauty is in our plurality, not in sameness.

It is customary in many offices and workplaces to assign a common dress code or a uniform. It is useful in developing professionalism and a sense of identity. But, what if the dress code enforcement does not allow a Sikh employee to wearing turban, or a Hindu employee from wearing saffron Tilaka or a Muslim employee from wearing head scarf? People's beliefs, cultural differences and values must be respected. A wise management should be able to tolerate differences and so should be each one of us. We should be able to follow the example of Ram's colleagues who were tolerant enough to understand and accept their friend's beliefs without any judgmental treatment. Compulsion is antithesis to pluralism.

> "Our ability to reach unity in diversity will be the beauty and the test of our civilization."
>
> - Mahatma Gandhi

What do you think about a culturally diverse society? What do you prefer, a homogeneous society or a pluralistic society? On a scale of 1 to

5, with 1 being the *least tolerant* and 5 being the *most tolerant*, what might be your score? What are the steps that you should take to score five?

> "Respect diversity, it's a strength, not a weakness."
>
> \- Muneer Amayoor

89 UNDERSTAND YOUR CHILD

What do you teach your children? Are you worried only about their marks in exams? Do you judge your child based on his I.Q. alone?

"Listen to me dear students. Today is a big day in your life. Today's exam will decide your future. The test will decide whether you are a winner or loser in your life! Pay close attention to what I am going to say. The exam is simple. To pass the test, you only have three tasks to finish. The three tasks are, flying from this rock to the yonder tree, burrowing a hole in the ground and swimming across this pond. Any doubts?"

Sitting on a high rock, the monkey teacher gave instructions to his student. Listening to his each word with utmost attention were his three young students, a sparrow, a rat and a fish. The students knew that so much was at stake and were determined to pass the test.

"Should we pass in all three tasks, sir", asked the sparrow.

"Yes, you should pass in all three of tests. Is everything clear now?", the monkey teacher replied. "Ok, let's get the ball rolling, the first test will be for the rat. Hey rat, come to the fore."

The rat knew that this exam is the most important milestone in his life. As he walked to the fore, his teacher's words vaguely echoed in his ears,"The test will decide whether you are a winner or loser in your life!" His heart was pounding crazy as he heard his teacher announce,"Your first test is flying test. You have five minutes to fly from here the yonder three. Your time starts....now!"

The rat climbed onto a high rock and jumped as far as he can, he tried flapping all his legs to keep him afloat. But, everything that goes up, should come down, unless it is bird. The rat fell down almost two feet away from the rock and rolled down the slop sustaining several cuts and bruises. The rat did not give up, he scrambled onto the rock again and as you might have guessed, the same repeated. The rat was tired, it was gasping for breath, he had bleeding through his cuts and as he was about to make the final attempt, he could hear his teacher announce, "Time up". The rat failed in the first test. Without amble time to rest, the teacher called him to perform the second test, swimming across the pond. After the teachers' signal, he jumped into the pond and tried swimming across. Though he managed to stay afloat for a while, he felt that he was going to drown. He immediately made his way back to the shore. He tried again. But he was wet, he was tired, he barely had time to rest after the first test, blood was oozing out through his cuts and he failed in his second test too. Then came the third and final test, burrowing half a meter into the ground in three minutes' time. He and his kin were born to do it, he had learned everything about burrowing from his elder brother. With a great level of confidence, he started digging through. At first, it seemed to work fine, he was making headway fast enough. But by the time, half the work was done, his arms began to give away, his fingers could not move anymore, his body heat shot up, so did his heart beat, he felt like being hit by a thunderstorm and collapsed to the ground before he can finish his task. He had passed out.

His teacher poured water on his face and as he gradually opened his eyes, he could see a blurred figure of a monkey and a sparrow watching over him. The sparrow said, "wake up rat, wake up, what happened to you? You failed even burrowing? What happened?" The vague and blurred figure of his teacher walked away from him and he heard his teacher announce, "the rat, he is a loser, I knew he would lose. HE IS A LOSER"

Can you guess, what would have happened when the fish was asked to fly from the cliff, burrow a hole and then to swim? What about the fate of little sparrow which was asked to swim first, then to burrow and then fly? Obviously, all the three students failed in all the three tasks. They were exhausted from the test after test that were impossible for them to accomplish.

Often, our education system works exactly like the exam in the jungle. Every child is forced to learn the same texts and develop the same skills and undergo the same tests. The fact that each child is unique is often overlooked. One may be good in Mathematics while another child can be excellent in communication skills and another at singing. You cannot make all of them engineers, nor can you make all of them a news reporter. All three of them can never be forced to become a pop singer. Instead of pushing every child through the same path, our education system should focus on identifying children's innate talents and nurturing them. A parent should not try to impose his/her unaccomplished dreams on a child. Instead, a parent needs to be a guide and a loving mentor. Along with nurturing children's innate talents, we should also try to inculcate values in them.

Here is a letter Abraham Lincoln wrote to his son's teacher.

My son starts school today. It is all going to be strange and new to him for a while and I wish you would treat him gently. It is an adventure that might take him across continents. All adventures that probably include wars, tragedy and sorrow. To live this life will require faith, love and courage.

So dear Teacher, will you please take him by his hand and teach him things he will have to know, teaching him – but gently, if you can. Teach him that for every enemy, there is a friend. He will have to know that all men are not just, that all men are not true. But teach him also that for every scoundrel there is a hero, that for every crooked politician, there is a dedicated leader.

Teach him if you can that 10 cents earned is of far more value than a dollar found. In school, teacher, it is far more honourable to fail than to cheat. Teach him to learn how to gracefully lose, and enjoy winning when he does win.

Teach him to be gentle with people, tough with tough people. Steer him away from envy if you can and teach him the secret of quiet laughter. Teach him if you can – how to laugh when he is sad, teach him there is no shame in tears. Teach him there can be glory in failure and despair in success. Teach him to scoff at cynics.

Teach him if you can the wonders of books, but also give time to ponder the extreme mystery of birds in the sky, bees in the sun and flowers on a green hill. Teach him to have faith in his own ideas, even if everyone tell him they are wrong.

Try to give my son the strength not to follow the crowd when everyone else is doing it. Teach him to listen to everyone, but teach him also to filter all that he hears on a screen of truth and take only the good that comes through.

Teach him to sell his talents and brains to the highest bidder but never to put a price tag on his heart and soul. Let him have the courage to be impatient, let him have the patience to be brave. Teach him to have sublime faith in himself, because then he will always have sublime faith in mankind, in God.

This is the order, teacher, but see what best you can do. He is such a nice little boy and he is my son."

Now, ask yourself, what do you expect the education to do for your child. Will your plans for your child help him/her be what they really want to be? Have you ever tried to find out that innate talent in your child? What can you do to nurture it?

"Let your child find the gem within."

- Muneer Amayoor

90 PHONING ETIQUETTE

When my wife had a terrible head ache and nausea, she called my friend who was a doctor. Even though he was driving to his clinic, he answered the call and gave her necessary directions. When I came to know about it, I told her, "You shouldn't have called him at that time. I know that you called, because you were ill. However, before calling someone, you need to consider the busy schedule they might have. It's OK if you have a really emergency message to pass."

She understood my point and nodded her head.

> "The two most powerful warriors are patience and time."
>
> - Leo Tolstoy

Let us have an introspection now. When you feel like ringing someone, do you ever pose to reflect if it is the right time to call? If someone does not attend the call, what do you do usually? Do you repeatedly call them until they pick your call? Or do you wait for some time and call them again? Always, the best idea is to let them return your call. When you call someone, do you have the habit of asking them if it is a convenient time to talk? When you call someone busy, do you try to limit the duration of your call? Don't we tend to overlook these matters?

Cell phones have made phone calls easily accessible. You need not run to the room where the landline connection is kept, you need not go through the telephone directory to dial. Your mobile phone is always an arm's length away. It does not mean that you can call anyone at any time you choose. Isn't it time to reconsider our phoning culture?

> "Owning a cell phone does not mean that you are free to ring anyone at any time of your choosing."
>
> \- Muneer Amayoor

91 DON'T CLIP THEIR WINGS

"A peacock feather is up for sale..., A peacock feather in exchange for a white pencil. Come, it's cheap"

"Who needs a red pencil? Come and grab it in exchange for a blank white sheet."

"Who has a piece of blue chalk? I can exchange it for my marble. Who needs a marble?"

You might think that a prehistoric barter-trade is in full swing here. Well, it is not an ancient market. Nor are there accomplished traders selling their produce. The scene is from my second-grade classroom where a system of barter-trade was in place. Most valuable commodities traded included pencils, feathers, plants, leaves, pieces of chalk, marble, pages ripped from the notebooks and such. However, the most valuable commodity was a special kind of leaf called "Ilammappotti" in my vernacular Malayalam. The specialty of this leaf was that if kept safe for some days, it would sprout tiny roots and leaves, making it look like a plant.

Naturally, these leaves were much in demand and I happened to have a big collection of it. By the standards of the trade, I was respectably rich!

One day, during a free period, the trade was in full swing and the sellers were all around the class. I was trading my collection of the "Ilammappotti" leaves for pencils along with some other classmates who were trying to trade their own commodities. All of a sudden, the headmistress of our school appeared out of nowhere, she was wielding a stick with which she used to punish "guilty" students. She was notorious for her discipline enforcement strategies. She used to ruthlessly punish students. In an instant, the traders bounced back to their respective seats, everyone stopped talking, the class turned silent. The teacher, in her shrill voice yelled at everyone and asked each one of us to return to where we were and resume whatever business we were engaged in before she entered the class.

"This class is a shame! Where do you think you are? It's a school, not a market", she said,"everyone, do as I say, return to wherever you were before I came and continue doing exactly what you were doing!"

The order seemed strange, yet, the frightened students, including me went back to the same places and acted like we were trading our commodities.

"I see, this is what you're up to. You want to turn this fine school into a filthy market where these craps are sold. Is this why you come here? Why.....? Why am I wasting my time..? Let me get it done. Well, extend your hands, I shall pay you for your hard work. I will pay you more than you deserve"

You can guess what happened next. She rounded up the little traders and with her stick, beat them hard until they cried.

The memories of this incident are still afresh in my mind. But was the way the teacher handled the situation, right? To find the answer, let me dissect the incident. Read on:

1) Was there a crime committed?

Yes. There was a crime. It was committed not by the students, but by the headmistress herself. What is her duty? To make sure that the teachers reach the school on time and teach the students according to the time table? Why was there no teacher in my class in the first place? If a teacher was sent to the class on time, wouldn't we be learning at that time? Who would reimburse the students for their wasted time? Why did the headmistress not send any teacher to our class?

2) If at all the students committed a crime, how grievous was it?

In the class students were engaged in conversations and their little trade. What is wrong with students finding ways to kill their time when the teachers concerned are not where they should be? Besides, with each trade deal and negotiations that the little traders make, wouldn't the students learn valuable lessons for their life?

3) What about the students' honesty?

When the teacher asked the students to return to their former posts, the kids could have simply lied and avoided the punishment. Instead, they chose to be honest and how did the teacher reward them for their honesty? What lesson did the students learn from the situation? It would go like this; "None cares about your honesty, none would appreciate your honesty, you better save yourself."

4) What about the punishment?

Why do some teachers still follow the medieval punishment methods to teach students of our time? Not only are the teachers' punishment strategies primitive they are morally repulsive as well.

5) The question of freedom and growth

Any individual's growth is intimately connected with the freedom he enjoys. Being free allows one to explore oneself and identify one's talents. The little trade could have been able to produce a future business magnet. Who knows!

In some schools, there is a practice of delegating class monitors to ensure class discipline. His/her duty is to write down the names of those who talked in the class when no teacher is in the class. Later the teacher would come and punish them. I strongly feel it is time we reinvented our classroom practices. Instead of curtailing their freedom, students should be taught to carry out their needs, talk to each other and build social relations, engage in healthy discussions, explore their own talents and weave their own dreams. Everyone does not have to be doctors and engineers. No trade should be ridiculed, everyone should be taught to respect all sorts of trade. Students should be given amble freedom to find the fields where they are talented. Most importantly, education should, in no way, clip their wings.

> **"If children feel safe, they can take risks, ask questions, make mistakes, learn to trust, share their feelings, and grow."**
>
> **- Alfie Kohn**

What would you have done if you had witnessed the barter system in our school? How will you use it as an opportunity to give insights and encourage the students?

> "Freedom is the first requirement for productive learning."
>
> \- Muneer Amayoor

92 SPREAD YOUR WINGS

"I've a good news and a bad news for you. The good news is that you've overcome the most critical stage, you will live. The bad news is that your body is completely paralysed. You are bed-redden for the rest of your life"

Imagine a doctor breaking this news to you. Well, that is exactly what happened to my friend, Raees Hidaya, when he regained his consciousness after spending several days unconscious in the ICU. Now, the same Raees Hidaya is a beacon of hope for many as he runs an NGO for helping similar people. During the 2019 flood that devastated Kerala, he helped coordinate a network of volunteers whose service helped many people to get back to life after being hit by the flood.

I had interviewed him for my show "Blooming Dreams" in All India Radio. He is a young energetic leader. When he was just sixteen years old, a tragic accident happened. On a fateful day, he met with an accident and he was badly injured. When he was lying unconscious in the road, somebody took him to the hospital. He was lying unconscious in the ICU for the next few days. After a few days of intensive treatment, he came to and the doctor explained the full extent of his injury. He was completely paralysed below his neck.

Never before had he thought that he would have to live his life confined to a bed. But, it is the reality now and he cannot run away from it. He lost all hope in life and his days seemed darker each day. He was hospitalised for a few months and he could not help thinking why the God was so cruel to him. In the room filled with the aroma of medicines, he could find no solace.

One day, lying in his hospital bed, staring at the sealing, his eyes happened to fall on an elderly man admitted in the same ward as him. He noted that not a single person ever visited the ill old man. Not even his sons and daughter. At the same time, Raees was always surrounded by people who came to visit him. His friends, relatives, people from his native village, his teachers and lot many others came to support him. But, what about the old man? With none ever to visit him, the old man's life was nothing less than a lonely hell. A wave of thought flashed across his mind, "How lucky I am to have a great company of all these loving people. Compared to the old man, I'm in paradise". His gratitude-cells awakened. As you know, there is no better medicine than being able to appreciate and be grateful for what one has. Now he knew his worth, his fortune and the life did not seem as dark anymore.

After treatment for a few months, he was discharged from the hospital. He was advised to do Physiotherapy on a regular interval. At the clinic, once he came across another patient who did not even have ₹ 2 to pay at the counter. Moved by the man's pathetic financial condition, he was overwhelmed by a sense of gratitude for what he has.

"How grateful should I be for what I have? Even though my parents are not very wealthy, we have enough money to make our both ends meet." This thought haunted him like a ghost and the ghost turned him to a brand-new person, a person grateful for the little he has and willing to do everything he can to make others' life little less unbearable.

If somebody needs blood, or if someone needs a walking stick or water bed, the first phone to ring in his village would be of Raees. He cannot even hold his phone in his hands, and yet each day he receives several calls seeking his help. Usually, with his brother's help he would talk to the people over the phone, and lying in his bed, he would coordinate a network of volunteers and philanthropists to help people in need. Remember, he is completely paralysed, he cannot even sit and yet manages to make other people's life better.

When the state of Kerala in India was hit by a heavy flood both in 2018 and 2019, he and his team Green Palliative were there in the frontline in the flood mitigation operations. They launched their own system to coordinate rescue and relief operations.

You know one thing? During the radio show, I asked him whether he feels bad and prays to God to revert him to his old healthy state. You will find it hard to believe his reply.

"Wouldn't it be ungrateful on my part, if I ask God to take back my current condition which has made me realise my true self?" I was taken aback by his reply and was left speechless.

It does not end there. If there is any protest for human rights and environmental justice, he would be there in the frontline of the protest as well. Lying in his wheeled bed, he would arrive in a van. Once at the protest ground, a man told him "It seems, you're at the wrong place my friend". He just smiled and replied he was there to protest for environmental cause.

I will not blame you if you find the next sentence hard to believe. Raees Hidaya is a traveler too. Often, with the help of his friends and relatives, he visits tourist places including some mountain tops! He likes to take a breath of fresh air sitting on the top of hills and behold the sunset from there. My friend, it is not over yet, he acts as a counselor to those who feel down after some traumatic events. With his empathetic talk, he has lifted many from the deep pits of darkness and transformed hundreds of lives. As you read his story now, he might be helping people in need.

> "As we express our gratitude, we must never forget that the highest appreciation is not to utter words but to live by them."
>
> - John F. Kennedy

Are you bed-ridden? Most probably, you are not. Can you name ten patients you helped? Can you list out five protests against human rights abuse or environmental injustice, in which you took part? Can you name any rescue operation you have been a part of? If you cannot, read this chapter again and you would know what you should do.

> "To grow beyond your tiny shell, be grateful for what you are."
>
> - Muneer Amayoor

93 SMILE OF TRUST

"She can't recognise me or my children. But, we don't care; I visit her whenever I can. Even if she doesn't recognise us, we know who she is, right? That's enough."

This is the usual reply from my neighbour if whenever she is asked about visiting her grand grandmother who is now in her 90s. The grand old lady is now suffering from Alzheimer's and could not recognise anyone. "Who are you?" she would ask everyone. Even her own children who take care of her have to introduce themselves a couple of times every day. Alzheimer's has nibbled into her memories. However, she smiles happily when her children and grandchildren are around.

Promises are to be kept, even if the other party does not remember it. Even if your friend dies, aren't you obligated to keep the promises you had given him/her? Before Alzheimer's took a toll on her memory, she had loved to be in the company of her loved ones. She had asked everyone to visit her all the time and share love. Since then, her memory has died out. She could not even recognise her own children. Yet, to this day that word is kept by all her children and grandchildren. They sit around her and talk. They try to make her happy in whatever way they can. That's life. That's the value of the promises.

> "Keep your promises and be consistent. Be the kind of person others can trust."
>
> – Roy T. Bennett

Do people take your promises seriously? If "Yes", great. If "No", why? What can you do about it?

> "Do not make any promise, if you are not sure that you can keep it."
>
> - Muneer Amayoor

94 WHAT DO YOUR CHILDREN NEED?

What's the most important element for a tree? Fruits? Flowers? Leaves? Trunk? Branches? Roots? or anything else? Before reading on, give it a thought.

Flowers add beauty. Fruits give tasty output. Without leaves, no photosynthesis will take place. If there is no trunk, can the tree stand tall? Branches make it allow it to trap more sun's energy. Now, what about roots? The tree gets water and nutrients through the root. Besides, it is the roots that hold the tree in place. Now, you might think that the roots are the most important elements for a tree to thrive. Are they?

OK, now, think again. Is there anything more important than the roots for the trees? Yes, it is the environment. Without the right surroundings, no tree will survive. Right soil, right amount of sunlight, water, climate and such are the crucial elements for a tree to survive. What use do the roots have if the soil is poor in quality? Without a good surrounding, will the tree be able to develop a big trunk, big branches, leaves or fruits? No.

> "Children are like wet cement whatever falls on them makes an impression."
>
> - Haim Ginott, child psychologist

Bombarding your kids with all the resources in the world will not help them. Make sure that they have the right surroundings to grow. What they need the most is an environment where they are free to ask questions, to act little naughty, make friends, make mistakes, talk to animals and flowers and play with kids and adults. An inspiring environment and a pair of free wings are the greatest gifts that you can give your children.

> "You are a product of your environment."
>
> - Muneer Amayoor

95 LITTLE QUARRELS

"A ticking time bomb that could explode any moment." This is how Alfred's neighbour, Joe, describes Alfred's house. Not because some nefarious gang have planted a time-bomb in Alfred's home. But, when Alfred and his wife Annie are both home, every day, they would find some reasons for a nasty squabble. Though there would not be much of a reason for the quarrel, usually, their yelling could be heard a mile away. Sometimes, the quarrel even escalates to a fist-fight, making the neighbours concerned. "Hey, what is going on there, Annie", Joe would ask through his window when the quarrel seems to get out of control. "You mind your own business, Joe", Alfred would yell back.

Caught in between the two quarrelling spouses is their five-year old son, Alex. Most days, he wakes up to see his parents quarrel with each other. Every time, they quarrel, the frightened poor boy would run down to the basement, where in a corner he would sit with his head buried in his folded hands. Many nights, he would fall asleep, alone, sobbing and tears running down his face. Moreover, alarmed by his strange bullying behaviour and poor performance, his nursery teacher had called Annie several times.

If this was to continue, how will it affect little Alex? Is he likely to be a smart and studious child? Will he have a normal childhood? Will it affect his emotional and cognitive development? Will he grow up to be a respected and valuable member in the society?

> "If there are quarrels between the parents, the ground will be prepared in their children for the severest predisposition to a disturbance of sexual development or to neurotic illness"
>
> - Sigmund Freud

It is quite normal to quarrel sometimes. Little quarrels can be instrumental in strengthening the relationship between partners. However, if it becomes a regular explosive routine, its effects on the partners and long-lasting impact on the children can be disastrous.

Now, what is your priority? Losing a minor quarrel with your spouse or losing your child's future?

> "It's okay to quarrel at times, but never okay to play with your kids' future."
>
> \- Muneer Amayoor

96 A TRIP WITH FAMILY

A few days after my marriage, the whole family went on a picnic. My spouse, Suhra, my father, mother, brothers, their wives and children-the whole crew was there. I remember, it was a pleasant evening on a riverbank. I particularly remember a tree by the riverside. It was a tree with a special S-shaped branch. I sat on this natural swing and invited Suhra to sit by my side. The branch was strong enough to support us both. Besides, like a swing, the branch could move back and forth. Much like a cinematic scene, the newly-wed couple swayed back and forth on branch against the beautiful backdrop of a grassy riverside. The camera crew, my brothers and children holding their mobile cameras, shot the scene from all directions and the crew was grateful for the unexpected romantic scene they could shoot.

But, what good is a film without an unexpected twist?! Right? The video crew's wish was granted when I attempted to move a bit backward to get more comfortable with my sitting and the miserable fate befell. Alas! I slipped from the branch and the next thing I remember is dangling from the branch upside down. As one of the children commented later, I looked like a bat. Somehow, I had managed to cling onto the branch with my legs holding tight around the branch.The scene took a sudden, drastic change from the romantic to the adventurous. At the first moment, everyone rushed towards me, genuinely concerned for my safety. But, once it was clear that I was safe, fear and concern gave way to a loud burst of laughter. Everyone laughed their head out, my newly-wed wife hid her giggle under her kerchief. And I too laughed, to be more precise, giggled out of my embarrassment.

Moments with family are great.They form ever shining memories to cherish in our heart. If you go for a short walk with your spouse or elderly father and mother, or with your brothers and sisters, along with strengthening your bond, it will invigorate you in a special way. Family time can be leisure time too.

> "Sometimes you will never know the value of a moment until it becomes memory."
>
> - Dr.Seuss

When was the last time you went on a trip with your whole family- mother, father, spouse, children and everyone else? When are you planning for the next trip?

"To strengthen your roots, find occasional free time to go on a trip with your family. What good is a giant tree if its roots do not run deep?"

- Muneer Amayoor

97 APPRECIATE THE BLESSINGS IN YOUR LIFE

Are you able to stand on your feet and take care of yourself? Most probably you are. Of 1440 minutes a day, how many minutes do you spend feeling genuine empathy for the less fortunate people around you?

At All India Radio, Manjeri, we had a special live phone-in programme in connection with the lock-down imposed at the time of Covid-19 pandemic. The programme named "Veettuvishesham" (roughly translated as Household Tidings) was meant for people to have a small-talk with us when they were stuck at home. One day, when I was sitting in the studio with my colleagues, we got a call from a young lady. She sounded quite energetic and excited to have a chit-chat with us. During the conversation, she revealed that she was suffering from Osteogenesis Imperfecta from birth. It is a genetic condition where the bones are so fragile that they are broken so easily. Because of the condition, she could not walk; walking is too hard on her bones that they will instantly break into pieces if she tried. To move from one place to another, instead of walking, she has to slide on her buttocks. During our conversation, she also told us about her brother, who was also born with the same condition. His condition is even more severe and to move around he cannot even slide on his buttocks. Instead, has to literally roll his body to move from one spot to another. A person who has to crawl or roll in order to move from point A to B, imagine. We then spoke to him. I will never forget that short conversation. Just like his sister, he shared a lot of things with a lot of energy and affection. It was only with great sense of disbelief that, I was able to digest the idea that these two siblings who sounded simply awesome and more vibrant than most of us, were actually suffering from a condition that many of us cannot even dare to imagine.

Awesome! Unbelievably awesome! I cannot find another word to describe these incredibly resilient siblings with a morale of steel. The story does not end there. With every sentence, they kept on giving us little doses of shock.

The biggest shock wave was yet to come. While talking, the brother happened to share his biggest worry, with us. Believe it or not, their biggest worry was not about themselves, not about their parents, not about their future. More than being concerned about their own condition and absolute inability to move, they were concerned about the ordinary people who were most hit by the lock-down. They were weeping for the people who, due to the lock-down, may have lost their jobs, small business that were forced to shut, people who lost their livelihood and the migrant workers walking miles on an empty stomach.

Overwhelmed by a sudden sense of respect, affection and admiration for the siblings, my colleagues and I sighed in total disbelief. I, personally, hung my head in shame.

Yes, such people do exist-people who restore our faith in humanity, people who can think beyond their own everyday troubles and show genuine empathy for others' suffering. People like these siblings, who can fully appreciate what they have and what they are rather than wining about what they do not have and what they are not, teach us a profound lesson. Everything does not have to be self-centerd. Our thoughts, our fears, our concerns, our complaints, our aspirations and everything could grow out of our own little world, provided we are able to fully appreciate everything we have. Ability to genuinely empathise with others' is the yardstick to weigh and judge one's character.

> **"What seems to us bitter trials are often blessings in disguise."**
>
> **– Oscar Wilde**

Can you count the blessings in your life? Start making a list. You can see, you can hear, you have a home, you can read this, you can write..... the list will be infinitely long. Why worry then? Start celebrating every moment of your life and learn to appreciate what you have.

> **"Count the blessings in your life, you will realize that the list is infinite."**
>
> **-Muneer Amayoor**

98 THE FINAL SMILE

After your death, imagine, what if your soul could linger around your body and be a witness to your funeral? What will your soul hear in the chatters at your home? Will the people mourn your death, or will they celebrate it silently?

Let me recall an incident my friend had told me. When a man, abruptly, breathed his last, his wife did not shed a drop of tear for him. Far from shedding tears for him, as soon as his body was cremated, she piled up all his belongings, burned them to ashes and took a relieving bath from the nearby river. It was the first night she slept peacefully after their marriage. As the life with him was a hell for her, his sudden departure was a welcome event for her. She was freed from the shackles and her children no longer had to sleep through nights of terror. Can there be worse fate than your death being treated as a blessing?

You and I have no guarantee that how long we are going to live. Whether it is short or long, what matters is the contributions we make to this world. If you could wipe tears from at least one person's eyes, then your life will be meaningful and there will be at least that one person who would genuinely shed tears for you when you breathe your last. Sometimes, people realise the value of a person only after their death. There are many people who help, empower and uplift those around them without anyone else's knowledge. They expect nothing in return, no favour, no fame, no power. They believe that the purpose of their life and the key to happiness in their life is making persons around them happier. When such a person departs from the earth, the future will feel dark for the people who depended on them.

> "It is not length of life, but depth of life."
>
> \- Ralph Waldo Emerson

Now, close your eyes and visualise, your body wrapped up in the white cloth. Visualise the people around. Can you see a blessed death with so many eyes shedding tears and so many hands raised to heaven, praying for you? The more impact you make on the world, the more people would mourn your death.

> "Blessed are those whose demise causes a flood of tears"
>
> \- Muneer Amayoor

99 SAY 'NO' TO 99

"Steve... that boy has his fingers in every pie. He is an asset for the college"

This is his how Steve's teacher commented about him once.

When there is a formal event at the college, the college authority need not worry about photography. Steve, will skip one or two periods and cover the event. If one of his friends' motor bike breaks down, Steve will arrive to their rescue with a couple of tools. In a few minutes, the bike will be good to go. He has a YouTube channel as well. It is called "Steve's Kitchen" where he uploads his cooking videos and food reviews. Often, when his teachers have any trouble with their laptop while making presentations, teachers would say, "Steve, can you take a look at it? Something is wrong". Besides, during the college tours and family gatherings, he entertains everyone with his songs. He did not make it to the college choir team though. However, what pushes him forward is the words of appreciation he receives from those around him. He is a 23 year old undergraduate and many of his classmates are also like him, really multi talented young girls and boys.

If you are a manger, entrepreneur, salesman, student, housewife or a layman, there is no argument that multiple talents will make you more handy and competitive. A bank manger should not only know how to manage accounts. If he knows the art of dealing with people, little computer repair, little bit of car mechanics and such, he would surely be able to take care of himself for most little troubles. Even if his car breaks down on the way to the bank, he could manage to repair it and reach the office on time. If the computer stops working while the technician is away, he will not have to regret if he is handy with computers. If he loves to sing, let him sing at home to relieve from stress and fatigue.

Now, let us consider the other side of the story. It is great to be a jack of all trades, but is that enough to be one of the most successful people or leaders? If you take a handful of most successful persons, you might note that there is something common among all of them. What is that? He/she will be a master in one field. Consider Sir Richard Branson. He knows everything there is to know about entrepreneurship and it is not a wonder that he is one of the most successful business men ever. Take

J K Rowling. She weaves spellbinding stories, and naturally, she is one of the most popular authors of the contemporary times. Les Brown, a master at motivating people. Tom Hanks, who, rather than acting in front of the camera, lives his characters, is one of the greatest actors of all time. Take great Albert Einstein now. He was not a jack of all trades. He was a master in Physics and naturally, his genius was recognised by the Nobel Prize he won.

Now, what does it take to become a master in ONE field? It's to say 'NO' to 99. What do I mean by that? Well, in order to become an expert in ONE field, you have to say 'NO' to 99 options out of 100. Let me break it down for you. Let us go through Steve's own life for that. Read on.

When you have too many options to choose from, it is really hard to make a choice. Despite all the appreciations Steve receives, he is not an expert in any of the fields he seems to excel. Well, it appears that Steve is talented enough to cover an event in his college. Yet, none of his photos have ever been published in any photographic journals. Besides, Steve has never won any prize in any photography competitions in his college or anywhere else. In fact, he is not a talented photographer though he thinks of himself as one.

- Now, why does Steve think that he is a good photographer?

Well, for the college, he is only a cost-effective means of covering the events at college. However, his teachers and the college authority are generous with their appreciations. Moreover, whenever he posts pictures on Instagram, given that he is a popular student in the college, he receives a lot of likes and positive comments. With every like and appreciations he receives, he becomes more and more happy and he is lead to think that he is, indeed, a great photographer, when he is actually not.

- How/why Steve's brain tricks him into thinking that he is a great photographer?

Here, the villain is Steve's own mind. His brain tricks him into thinking that he is a great photographer. How does that happen? Your brain is always thirsty for Dopamine, the happiness hormone we had mentioned in an earlier chapter. Dopamine gives you instant gratification and by doing so, it makes you biased. How did it work for Steve? Whenever he posted a picture on Instagram, he received so many likes and more followers, most of whom where his own college-mates and friends. The increasing number of likes makes him high on Dopamine. The high Dopamine coursing through his blood vessels gives him a sort of instant gratification. As a result, his brain gets addicted to the photography and makes him biased towards the same field. "Well, this is great. Let me post more photos. I'm indeed a great photographer", Steve's mind would say.

This is how Steve came to think that he is good at photography. The same story is true for how he became a handy mechanic for his teachers and friends. Same is true for how he came to think of himself as a good singer. His brain tricked him into thinking that he was an expert photographer, talented singer, handy mechanic and a talented chef. In reality, he was only a mediocre singer, a mediocre cook, a mediocre photographer and a mediocre mechanic.

Top leaders and most successful people are not mediocre in their field, they are experts. To become a top leader, to reach the zenith of success, identify a narrow niche for you and dig deeper and deeper until you know everything about that niche. Be an expert in Artificial intelligence, not a generalist in computer science. Be an expert actor, singer, painter or anything depending on your most valuable skill. Does it mean that you should not do anything other than that? Absolutely not. You can be an expert in a field and still be good in others fields. It is perfectly okay to be so. The alphabet "T" is a good model here. The alphabet "T", is made up of two lines, a vertical line and a horizontal line on its top. The horizontal line could represent your overall knowledge and awareness. Your overall knowledge and awareness does not have to go deep. In every field, you can try to develop a basic surface-level knowledge. The vertical line, which represents your area of expertise, should go deep under the surface. Unlike the horizontal line which maintains a consistency, the vertical line should go deep beneath the surface. In the shape of the alphabet "T", develop a deep knowledge in one field while developing an overall idea about everything else.

Why should you follow the model of "T"? Well, here it is. Keep reading. The "T-model" makes you a STUPID? Yes, you read it right. Before you give me that look, see what STUPID stands for. Here, STUPID stands for Smart Talented Unique Person in Demand. Be a Smart, Talented, Unique, Person in Demand, do not be a mediocre jack of all trades.

> "Each man is capable of doing one thing well. If he attempts several, he will fail to achieve distinction in any."
>
> - Plato

Many job aspirants complain that they get no job even after having a pile of certificates. Why is it like that?

Imagine, a candidate has earned certificates in astronomy, photonics, electronics and many other fields, and another one has secured same number of certificates in different subtopics of astronomy. Imagine, if both these candidates attend an interview to fill the post of an Assistant Professor in Astronomy, who will get the job? The first candidate? The second one? Of course, the second one. Because, he is a master in the field. Unlike the other candidate, he is not a jack of all trades. Yes, to create demand for you, never under estimate the power of ONE. Let's rephrase the old saying "jack of all trades, master of none" into "jack of all trades, master of ONE."

> "A specialist in one particular area outweighs a generalist in hundred areas. Say NO to 99 areas to be an expert in ONE."
>
> \- Muneer Amayoor

See Yourself In A Mirror...

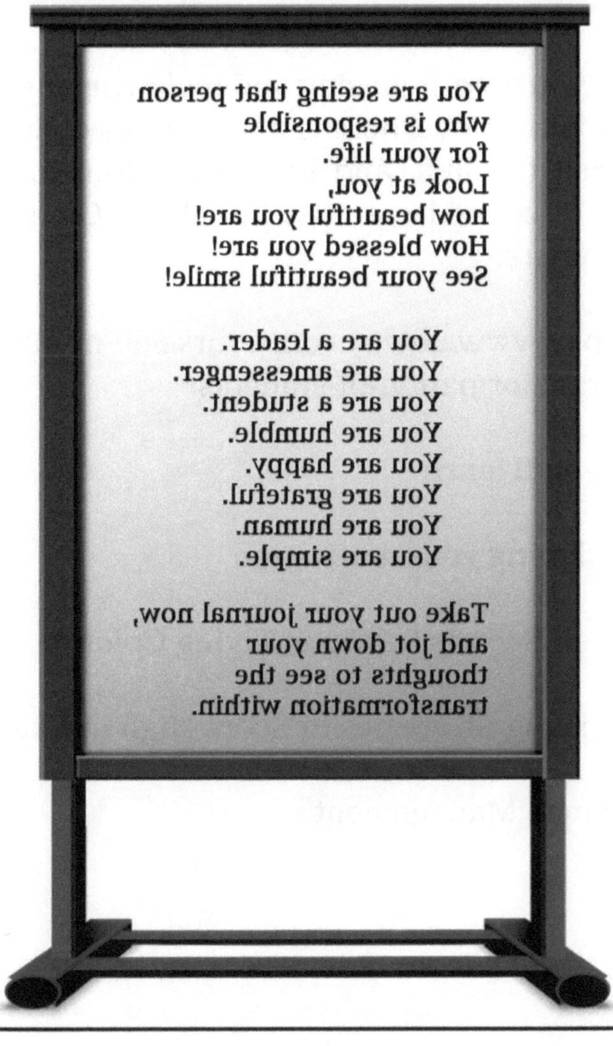

FREE BONUS 1

Thank you for purchasing and reviewing the book. As a token of love, here is a free bonus course for you. Visit the link, and enrol now. Join the tribe from 117 countries across the globe. Go, grab it. It's all yours.

https://www.udemy.com/course/60-minutes-to-total-transformation-of-students/

What you'll learn

- Designing your motivation
- Seven Secrets to Win in Flying Colours
- Learning Strategies to Score High in Exams
- Change Management

FREE BONUS 2

A surprise gift for you to expand your limits!

Visit: www.muneeramayoor.com/thegrowthhacker

Dear Friend

I request you to take just ONE MINUTE to leave an HONEST REVIEW on the Amazon website.

★★★★★

Please write down the key take-aways from the book and how it helped you in your transformation.

Remember

One thing

If you got any spark from this book, it is your duty to pass on the spark to at least ten people around you.

With love,
Muneer Amayoor

WHEN MUNEER AMAYOOR SPEAKS, EVERYONE GETS UNCOMFORTABLE

Because,

He pushes them out of their comfort zone, and helps them to engineer their life to grow beyond their imagination.

For getting him to push you and your team beyond the boundaries, mail at muneeramayoor@gmail.com

Mob: +91 9446393136
www.muneeramayoor.com

www.ingramcontent.com/pod-product-compliance
Lightning Source LLC
Chambersburg PA
CBHW050010170726
48282CB00025B/348
9788194951193